The
YELLOW ROSE
OF TEXAS

The
YELLOW ROSE
OF TEXAS

The Song, the Legend
and
Emily D. West

Lora-Marie Bernard

Foreword by James Glover

THE
History
PRESS

Published by The History Press
Charleston, SC
www.historypress.com

First published 2020

Manufactured in the United States

ISBN 9781467142571

Library of Congress Control Number: 2019951263

Notice: The information in this book is true and complete to the best of our knowledge. It is offered without guarantee on the part of the author or The History Press. The author and The History Press disclaim all liability in connection with the use of this book.

Dedicated to Jorie Nissen, Jennifer Parsley and Emily D. West.
The librarian, the historian and the brave ordinary woman
we will never really know.

I thank all three of them for enriching my life.

Contents

Foreword

The history of Texas, from earliest exploration up to the present day, is an epic saga composed of some of the most fantastic stories ever told. These stories have made their way into popular culture, patriotic platforms and songs and onto the silver screen. The more incredible tales usually are the ones with the most truth behind them; the underlying facts and conditions often are of more importance than the stories themselves.

The Yellow Rose of Texas is, in the vernacular of its telling, the story of a biracial slave girl captured by an invading Mexican army, conducted to the supreme commander's distinctly striped tent and ravaged by the depraved general. While he takes advantage of her, she returns the favor by distracting him from his duty and contributing to his ultimate downfall. The story of Emily Morgan, the property of Colonel James Morgan, has been taught in some form to almost every Texas school child since the 1930s. The Yellow Rose story is exciting, racy, salacious and largely an apparent work of fiction.

Our tale first emerges from the pages of William Bollaert's journals, penned during his Texas visit of 1842–44. Bollaert was an apt observer of customs, geography, politics and history. Prior to visiting Texas, he had traveled extensively throughout South America and Europe, publishing several works on a variety of topics, mostly for the British societies of which he was a member. Ostensibly, Bollaert had intended to publish his notes in manuscript form—he did begin work on such a manuscript at some point—but was distracted in other ventures, including the raising of a family.

Bollaert asserts that his story springs from a true and trusty gentleman, well placed in Texas politics, who was present at the Battle of San Jacinto. Most scholars who have researched Bollaert's papers agree that the source can be none other than then-president Sam Houston. Upon publication of Bollaert's work in 1956, under the title *Bollaert's Texas*, the Yellow Rose story was omitted as trivial and without substantial foundation. Nevertheless, the story had leaked out at least two decades earlier through scholars and researchers who had been mining the papers for information.

Had the tale made its appearance immediately following the 1836 battle, it would surely have been immensely popular, much as it was during the Texas Centennial of 1936.

In and of itself, the Yellow Rose story is a wonderful little tale comparable to something out of *The Arabian Nights*. From a standpoint of veracity, it has some issues. First, it is a single-source account that appeared several years after the events were to have taken place. The same problem arises when investigating Travis' Line in the Sand and the story of Francis Rose making his escape from the Alamo. These last two tales were published in an 1890s newspaper, as recounted by William Zuber, a veteran of the Texas Revolution. Some academics argue that his account is a ploy for recognition born of self-aggrandizement. Zuber didn't actually see the events take place; he wasn't there. Similarly, Houston was nowhere near Santa Anna's tent while the general was present and could not have seen anything relative to the Yellow Rose story, though he may have heard it from his men. He certainly would have been aware of the legal battle that followed—which is very relevant to the story and is covered in Ms. Bernard's present work. It is a bit odd that no one else recorded the story early on. Perhaps it was repeated to Bollaert to impress or entertain the visiting Englishman with no view to the details being exactly as they were presented.

The other problem with the story is that it makes some basic assumptions that have generally been accepted by the public and scholars alike. We are told that Emily is biracial and must have been a slave, as free blacks were very uncommon in Texas at that time. Indeed, the noble Texians who "rescued" her believed her to be a slave and intended to auction her along with Santa Anna's other possessions. This goes hand in hand with the presumptive reasoning behind her capture: that she was a slave and was therefore contraband, or illegal property, under the laws of Mexico because Mexico had outlawed the practice some years earlier. The third major assumption is that poor, promiscuous Emily had been "entertaining" the Mexican general in his tent— even by schoolchildren, this was interpreted in a salacious manner.

The Yellow Rose story actually reveals a great deal about race and race culture in the United States and England in the 1840s and how it had changed in Texas from the mid-1830s to the time Houston related his tale to Bollaert.

Mexican Texas in the 1830s was not a liberal utopia; several attempts by abolitionist societies to establish colonies in Texas were thwarted—one by Stephen Austin himself. It was, however, a mixed population, much as that of Mexico. The notable exception was that, aside from Nacogdoches and the San Antonio–Victoria area, very few Hispanic people made their home north of the Nueces River. With free people of color, it is a different story.

The term "free people of color" is a period term often denoted as "FPOC" on documents of the era and refers to blacks, mulattos or pretty much any admixture of Negro and white, Indian or Hispanic. While the number of free people of color in pre-revolution Texas is not staggering, it is far greater than what most of us have been led to believe. In other words, just because Emily was a mulatto does not indicate that she was a slave; she could just as well have been a free black.

Mexico never outlawed slavery while Texas was part of the republic. Plantations in the Yucatan, mines and ranches in Jalisco and the textile mills and cotton plantations of Puebla, near Mexico City, boasted large numbers of black and Indian slaves. The state of Coahuila, of which Texas was part, did make slavery illegal in 1830 but rescinded the law within six months of its passage; slavery was too important to the economy. The seizing of Emily must be seen in a different light. Rather than contraband, she was taken (for she says that she was taken) as something of value. The Mexicans obviously did not realize she may have been free. Santa Anna's officers, in the journals and diaries they left behind, tell of the treasures that were plundered from the Texas countryside. General Urrea, who occupied Columbia and Brazoria while Santa Anna was being "entertained" at San Jacinto, reportedly returned to Matamoros with three thousand head of cattle that he acquired during the Texas Campaign. Emily apparently was taken either to be a slave for her captors or to be sold as a prize. Whether she was free or not prior to her capture really would not matter much.

As to the entertainment part of our story, just what could that mean? Certainly, it could have the baser meaning most of us have accepted it to have. Or, since Emily was literate, could it simply mean that she was reading to the general or conversing about current affairs, as she was likely well read? Aside from those in Texas, all accounts of Santa Anna paint him as a very courteous gentleman. Emily was not Emily Morgan, the slave of Colonel James Morgan. Emily was very likely Emily West, a free person of color native to New York whom Morgan had hired as a teacher for his children. In any case, subsequent events prove that she was literate, intelligent and apparently knew her own will—and was accustomed to exercising it.

Race in the early nineteenth century was often a complex, sticky issue. In the northern United States, slavery was in a steep decline. The abolitionist movement was gaining ground, but questions remained about what to do with free blacks. In some cases, they were precluded from owning property. They did not generally associate freely with whites, and they often were not granted full citizenship—they could not vote, hold office, represent themselves in the courts or serve in the military. In Mexican Texas, race was not much of an issue, due in large part to the fact that Mexico, like most other former Spanish possessions, was a country of mixed races. Free people of color were on pretty much even footing with everyone else. Emily likely found employment in Texas hoping to land in a country where she had greater opportunities and more freedoms than in her native United States (at this point, we have no evidence that she was born other than free or in any country other than the United States). Immigration to Texas, seen in that light, makes perfect sense. Many other free people of color did the same.

Even before Austin established his first colony in 1821, free men of color crossed the Sabine River from western Louisiana in search of livestock. By the late 1820s and early 1830s, a sizable community of free people of color, mixed with whites and some French Creoles, settled in what would become Jefferson County, Texas. Among them were the Gallier, Walker, Hayes, Perkins, Ashworth, Bunch, Goings and Thomas families. Families of Perkins and Goings were well established in the Nacogdoches vicinity before the revolution. Even San Antonio had a small population of free people of color—largely because they were simply citizens with the same rights and responsibilities as everyone else.

Under Mexican rule, free people of color in Texas prospered. They conducted business in their own right, ran cattle (their own), bought and sold land and operated businesses. They also took part in public affairs, served in the military—even during the Texas Revolution—and owned slaves. Several instances are recorded of free men of color filing eligibility claims for land grants either as military service bounties or as headrights under the old empressarial system prior to Texas independence. A few are recorded as having received their headright grants. So far, research has not revealed any free women of color receiving land grants under the colonization laws, although several of their white counterparts (at least ten in Austin's first colony) did receive their own headright grants. Neither have the records revealed—thus far—free people of color voting in local elections during the Mexican era and certainly not in the early years of the republic.

The record does show that free people of color contributed to the Texas cause. Sam McCullough was likely the first person wounded in the struggle for independence. A musket ball pierced his shoulder during the taking of the presidio at Goliad in 1835, disabling him for life. Blacksmith Greenberry Logan was near Ben Milam during the final days of the siege of Bexar in December 1835. A sniper's ball cost him the use of an arm and his trade. William Goings operated a thriving mercantile business in Nacogdoches. He made treaties with the local Indians—notably Chief Bowles—to keep the peace during the revolution.

As a republic, the Texas constitution contained a provision requiring all free people of color to leave the country by 1842. Those failing to do so stood to forfeit any property they owned and would be subjected to stiff fines or even be forced into slavery. An additional provision stated that petition might be made to Congress for special permission to remain. As might be expected, more than sixty such petitions were entered, many with prominent white signatories affirming the character of the petitioners.

What might have sounded like a good idea when it was "those people" became something entirely different when it came to trusted business associates, family friends and patriots who had put their lives and property at hazard during the revolt.

Receiving a deluge of petitions, many signed by prominent men of the republic, Congress found it had more than it could handle. Rather than treat each petition individually, the governing body passed the Ashworth Act of 1840. Originally denoted as "An Act for the Relief of Certain Free Persons of Color," the Ashworth Act stated that free people of color who had been in Texas before March 2, 1836, and who had not stood against the revolution nor left the country during the conflict were entitled to remain—both the heads of household and their families. The act took the name of four of the specific individuals listed therein: William, Abner, David and Aaron Ashworth. Also specifically mentioned is Elisha Thomas, former brother-in-law and likely a cousin to the Ashworths. (It is noteworthy that the Ashworths were stock-raisers and supplied beef to the Texas army during the revolt and that both William Ashworth and Elisha Thomas had served in the Texas army in the months following San Jacinto to keep the peace in the area around Jasper County.)

What the Ashworth Act did not do was restore the rights and duties of citizenship to any of these people. Following passage of the act, the record shows a growing number of legal cases and congressional petitions for reinstatement of the rights of citizenship, such as representing oneself in a court of law, buying and selling property without prior approval, the ability to testify before legal bodies either on their own behalf or for others or service as jurors. Considering that many of these people were businessmen or tradesmen, the inability to file claims with the local courts without going through a "white man" was a distinct disadvantage.

With little sympathetic response from Congress, free people of color had to find a way to regain some of their lost rights and dignity. So began the practice of "passing," where those who were light-skinned enough would pass themselves off as whites. For those who were able, this worked fairly well; still, they at times encountered problems from those who "knew what they were."

With Emancipation in the late 1860s, the problems of free people of color intensified. Not only were they facing discrimination due to their skin color, but they also were viewed in the same light as the recently freed slaves. This intensified the move toward passing—again, for those who were able.

The Yellow Rose story, as originally related, doesn't amount to much more than a cute little tale that played into patriotic and political goals. Below the surface, the story of a free woman of color falling into misfortune while making her own way in the world actually has a great deal to show us.

—James Glover
Historic Site Manager, Stephen F. Austin–Munson County Park
Direct descendant of Elisha Thomas

Preface

You've heard about the legend. You've heard about the song. Now learn how the two met.

Inside every legend will be a messy load of opinion, interpretation and hard facts. The way these are sifted turns story into myth. In Texas, no better case study exists for this intellectual churning than the story of the Yellow Rose of Texas. From the early days of blackface performers to the twentieth-century musicals of Elvis Presley, Texans have lived with the Yellow Rose of Texas in one incarnation or another. Inside the story of Emily D. West and a minstrel song, we find a microcosm for the myth building that surrounds the Texas Revolution and our nation.

The legend catapults the story of a single woman's experience in a bloody revolution from obscurity to mainstream. Emily has been one of the most debated women in Texas history. Amateur, independent and academic historians, usually men, have interpreted, defended and fought for their interpretation of the research for decades. Many things are worth fighting for in Texas, and apparently, a legend is one of them.

This book traces the life of a woman who left scant trails about her existence. No one has a complete profile of Emily West, and no one probably ever will. Anyone who claims to know what she looked like is dreaming. No photos or detailed description of her features, size, weight or even skin color are known to exist, although she has been described repeatedly as mulatto or, as we say today, biracial. The song describes a woman like this, but not one single verifiable historical source can tell what Emily West looked like. Maybe she was biracial, maybe she wasn't. She was certainly a free black woman.

The Texas effort to confuse "fact with fable with song" has been so successful that no one can even tell the story about Emily West accurately. I don't even claim to do that. I will, however, claim to at least try to provide the most modern explanation about the life she lived and give some reasonable context for the decisions she might have made. I also give my best attempt to unravel the song and its journey to become a Texas anthem. I draw on primary sources whenever possible and secondary ones when I have nowhere else to go or I think the writer has compelling analysis. I need to give a great deal of credit to Phillip Thomas Tucker and his 2014 book *Emily D. West and the "Yellow Rose of Texas" Myth.*

I also give respect to those academics and historians who have sifted and sorted through the annals of Texas as best they could. It has become clear to me that they have dedicated large portions of their lives to preserving her legacy and the myth. Without them, I would not be able to reexamine her empowering biography and the great moment she encountered in Texas. Because of their contributions, I've been able to retrace a tale that transcends time. This myth still has modern relevance inside our national conversations about gender and race. The Yellow Rose of Texas legend made a free black woman part of a collective history through a song never written about her and a tale that was never intended to be published.

Few original documents have ever been found about Emily West. From these documents and a predominately male-driven narrative, she became embedded in Texas culture one hundred years after she lived. She became an exploited sex symbol because of a single interpretation at a specific moment in time. She was saddled with a characterization that has never been proven and probably never will be. She was given celebratory status for an event she never had any responsibility for creating. She has been remembered as a woman who gave all she had for Texas by having sex with a Mexican general. The implications of that highly charged tale became the crux for the legend. It was this moment of her life that defined her even though it was based in sheer speculation at best and a tawdry lie at worst. Little interpretation, meanwhile, has been given about why she would be anxious to leave the land she sacrificed her reputation for within sixteen months after it became a republic. This was the part of the tale that mesmerized me. I wanted to unravel why she would even bother to come to Texas just to leave it.

The intersection between her life and the song says more about who we were as Texans than it does about her illuminating experience. She was a single free black woman in both the North and the South during the pre–Civil War era. The world she lived in and the men she was connected to describe the ways the nation was manipulated and shaped by those who benefited from an economy fueled by dark-skinned people.

Many stories about the Yellow Rose of Texas have been written for the Texans who want to believe the standard myth. I do not wish to repeat those stories. I was raised as a Texan who knew them. Friday night football games often included a halftime routine to the catchy tune. As I child, I chose the yellow rose as my favorite flower solely because it had so many layers of meaning for a Lone Star woman. I honor the myth and story because it represents a time that our state and nation reflected it. Today, though, I've quit doing splits and high kicks in white boots on a football field. My Friday nights aren't spent in stadiums anymore, but I do understand why Texans want their sports fields so big. Roses aren't my favorite flowers, but I still appreciate them. I have grown just like Texas has. We can find new meaning in memories and grow without forsaking them.

This Yellow Rose story was written for the new Texan. This is for the Texan who never knew the origin of Emily and might learn something from it. Taken as a whole, her story shows us a deep and forgotten connection between New York and the Mexican territory. It tells us the lost story of the free black community and those who had a vision for a Texas very different from the one that it became. Those Texans who are already Lone Star proud, like me, might discover a new part of the state's history they might have never known. To start, I hope you learn that the song is not biographical. In fact, this Texas anthem was not written in Texas at all.

As you read these pages, I hope you are enlightened by a perspective never heard. I hope you appreciate the interpretation that bridges song and woman in ways never done before. I hope you discover an enduring captivation for the Texas spirit. Most of all, I hope you find a respect for Emily D. West that inspires you to seek your own modern Texas legends. I also hope you learn to appreciate legendary Texas heroes as real men and women who were shaped and created by the times they lived in and not by midcentury media or academic dalliances.

The truth about Emily D. West has so much more power, strength and courage than the myth. Let's honor her for what she really was: a single free black woman who survived a bloody war and a political system on her own terms. Let us transform the legend and begin a fresh conversation about the ways Texas was created and shaped by all of our experiences.

Cheers,
The Author

Acknowledgements

I must thank Jennifer Parsley and Michael Bailey for the hours on the phone and inside direct messages trying to wrap my head around the elusive Emily West and the characters who made her story. I hope the end result reflects the help and assistance they gave me. I have to say, Texas history is more fun when I'm playing with my friends.

I have to thank Jorie Nissen, who broached a discussion with me about Emily. She asked me to do some more research about her myth and present my findings at an upcoming program she was planning. I did and soon realized what she already knew: a new book about Emily and a new interpretation about her legend was long overdue. Without Jorie, this book wouldn't have happened. She saw it before I did.

My editor Ben Gibson was so patient during unexpected writer blocks. I don't have them often, but Emily gave me a few. This was our second book together, and I thank him for everything he does for me.

This is my third book for Arcadia/The History Press, and I want to thank the team and especially to senior editor Hilary Parrish. The publishing house has shown an enduring interest in my work, and I'm glad to be able to represent it and those who make history come alive for mainstream readers.

I feel like I should thank my brother, Robert. He likes Texas.

Finally, and forever, I thank Bobby Gervais. Nothing I do means anything without him. At the end of every book, I type my last word, say goodbye to the characters who lived so well inside my head and close the manuscript. Then, I return to daylight, where I find Bobby, standing firmly in the center of a world he built for me.

Chapter 1

The Roses of the States

In 1955, at the foot of the Robert E. Lee Monument in Dallas, the reigning beauty queen from the Tyler Rose Festival received a golden record of that year's most popular song. While Maymerle Shirley was being elevated from a regional to a statewide title, the local WBAP radio station described the scene of her coronation. The reporter announced over the airwaves: "Gals hand out confederate [*sic*] flags while Lee Park abounds in yellow roses."

Mitch Miller was an oboe player whose career spun him into an iconic music producer. He was also a music director. It was his orchestral rendition of the Lone Star song that knocked Bill Haley's "(We're Gonna) Rock Around the Clock" off its perch at the top of the bestseller's chart.

In 1955, "The Yellow Rose of Texas" captured the world's attention. People throughout the planet sung the song about the man who cried when he lost his woman. More than one million people bought copies.

To hold a beauty title in its name and to receive a golden disk of the song from Miller could easily have been one of the best dreams any Texas girl would have had. When Shirley died in June 2017, her obituary mentioned her as a true southern lady. Her golden disk represented the 5,000th copy made. She considered it a special honor from the man who created an unofficial Texas anthem.

Miller's song version was a cultural hit in Texas and Hollywood. The following year, the tune was featured in the movie *Giant* with Elizabeth Taylor and Rock Hudson. It reached the No. 1 spot in the United States on the same week that the movie's other famous actor, James Dean, died.

Miller, the New Yorker, may have led the charge that aligned the song with Texas pride, but Elvis Presley put the momentum on steroids. In 1964, the King donned a swanky ten-gallon cowboy hat for a dance scene in the movie *Viva Las Vegas* while he belted out new lyrics but kept the catchy tune. He changed the lyrics to include references to the Texas Panhandle and Metroplex cities, like Amarillo and Dallas. Presley released the tune again in 1969.

Bing Crosby also sang a rendition. Willie Nelson, Roy Rogers, Gene Autry, Pat Boone and a number of other artists sang versions of it. In 1984, Johnny Lee and Lane Brody released yet another version that reached the No. 1 spot for country music songs that year. In 1994, the TV miniseries *James A. Michener's Texas* resurrected Autry's version and used it on the soundtrack.

Like Presley's performance, other singers would change the lyrics, but the tune remained the same. Sometimes the lyrics hailed the romance of a lost

Above: Publicity photo of Mitch Miller and his television cast of dancers from the show *Sing Along with Mitch*. *Courtesy NBC Television.*

Opposite: "The Yellow Rose of Texas" record as composed by Mitch Miller. *Courtesy of Kahle/ Austin Foundation.*

love. Other times, they evoked modern Texas pride. In still other versions, they honored the fallen Confederacy.

Yet none of these singers was the first to bring an unofficial Texas anthem to the masses. The song might, in fact, be one of the most successful minstrel songs of all time, but it wasn't written as an anthem for anything. It wasn't even written in the South, much less in the Lone Star State. "The Yellow Rose of Texas" was written almost exactly one hundred years before Mitch Miller created his internationally renowned orchestral version of it. "The Yellow Rose of Texas" first hit the main stage when white men wearing blackface wrote and sang it in New York.

THE CHRISTY'S SKIT

Edwin P. Christy was the leader of the Christy's Minstrels. *From* Christy's Plantation Melodies.

In its original format, "The Yellow Rose of Texas" documents a sad, lonely plantation slave man who laments about the beautiful biracial woman he lost somewhere along the Rio Grande. Originally published in the 1800s in a seventy-page songbook from Pennsylvania, the song was part of a minstrel performance that also featured tunes like "See, Darkie, See," "Uncle Gabriel, the Darkey General" and "The Darkey Blackberrying Party."

No sheet music accompanied the original song, but it was part of an enormous song list for the Christy's Minstrels. The blackface six-member minstrel group was popular entertainment in the North's towns and villages. The men used burned corks to create the blackfaces and then acted out caricatures of enslaved Africans and northern "dandies." They performed original skits that featured song, dance, comedy and theater. The general intent of the troupe in pre–Civil War America was to bolster the slavery argument and present a picture that blacks would not want to come to the North even if they could because they deeply enjoyed southern culture and working on plantations.

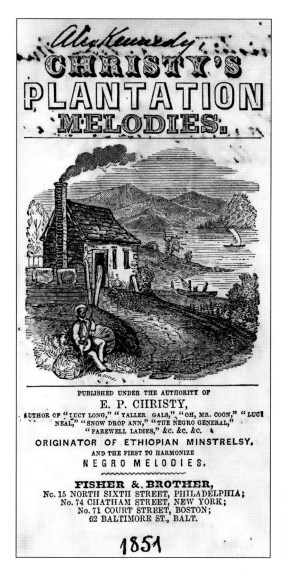

The cover of a *Christy's Plantation* playbook that would contain lyrics to songs the troupe composed. *From* Christy's Plantation Melodies.

"The Yellow Rose of Texas" originally appeared in 1853 on page 52 of Edwin P. Christy's *Christy's Plantation Melodies No. 2*. Its lyrics were part of what the Handbook of Texas described as a "fictional minstrelsy genre." At the time, the group sang a series that was described as "The Roses of States." In addition to "The Yellow Rose of Texas," other Christy songs included "The Virginia Rose-Bud," "The Rose of Baltimore" and "The Rose of Alabama." Most of the songs in the songbook, including "The Yellow Rose of Texas," don't feature composer credits. A few songs are clearly credited and mention an instrumental accompaniment, but it seems Christy or another troupe member chose to write this one uncredited, sans accompaniment. A composer credit would have meant little anyway. Christy kept all the rights to the troupe, the songs and the song list.

In 1858, a composer using the initials J.K. gave the song a revision. The identity of J.K. has been debated through the decades, but new research supports the idea that he was a Christy's Minstrels troupe member. In 2010, Joan Duffy, an archivist at the Yale Divinity School, uncovered documents supporting the theory that John Kelly was the mysterious composer. Kelly, a New Yorker, was a popular comedian who played the banjo and composed songs. He used the stage name J.K. Campbell in 1851 as part of the Christy's Minstrels. He kept that stage name until 1859, when he changed it to J.K. Edward. He changed his name at the request of other troupe members. It would initially seem that J.K. was updating "The Yellow Rose of Texas" for the series list, but he might not have been. The changes occurred five years after the song was written, so he might have simply done it to make the song useful in a different skit. He changed the references from the "yellow girl" to "yellow rose" and added a piano accompaniment. Given the timespan of Kelly's employment with the minstrels, he might have been the original composer as well.

His revised lyrics set the song to become a hit. The following year, Napoleon G. Gould updated the sheet music for the guitar, which delighted the publishers, Firth, Pond and Co. The publishing house printed twenty-two Christy's Minstrels songs by 1858 and was thrilled with the money it made from "The Yellow Rose of Texas." None of the other "Roses of States" songs ever reached the popularity of the Texas one. Song sheets were sold for twenty-five cents apiece, and an advertisement heralded its great appeal: "It is a most astonishing fact, that three thousand copies have been printed and sold of this pleasing song since the new year. The demand has in no wise abated, and we desire all our friends to purchase a copy at once."

J.K., or Kelly, might have been delighted that his new rendition was a pop hit, but he likely never expected it to become associated with Texas pride. Today, the original lyrics to "The Yellow Rose of Texas" are considered so racist that Connecticut College places a disclaimer on its digital library alerting a person that he or she is about to read some astonishing words. The site states, "Some of these resources may contain offensive language or negative stereotypes. Such materials should be seen in the context of the time period and as a reflection of attitudes of the time."

The 1853 lyrics of "The Yellow Rose of Texas" were:

There's a yellow girl in Texas
That I'm going down to see;
No other darkies know her,
No darkey, only me;
She cried so when I left her
That it like to broke my heart,
And if I only find her,
We never more will part.

Chorus: She's the sweetest girl of colour
That this darkey ever knew;
Her eyes are bright as diamonds,
And sparkle like the dew.
You may talk about your Dearest Mae,
And sing of Rosa Lee,
But the yellow Rose of Texas
Beats the belles of Tennessee.

Where the Rio Grande is flowing,
And the starry skies are bright,
Oh, she walks along the river
In the quiet summer night;
And she thinks if I remember
When we parted long ago,
I promised to come back again,
And not to leave her so.

Chorus: She's the sweetest girl of colour, &c

Oh, I'm going now to find her,
For my heart is full of woe,
And we'll sing the songs together
That we sang so long ago.
We'll play the banjo gaily,
And we'll sing our sorrows o'er,
And the yellow Rose of Texas
Shall be mine forever more.

Chorus: She's the sweetest girl of colour, &c.

For the next century, J.K.'s revised "Yellow Rose of Texas" lyrics would continue to be sung by white men, including mainstream entertainment legends like Gene Autry. No black men appear to have recorded the song.

It wouldn't be until the 1990s that blackface comic routines would die. The final community stage production of the genre that made African Americans a punchline happened in picturesque Vermont. The last major public blackface skit was in 1993, when actor Ted Danson wore blackface to the Friars Club with his date, Whoopi Goldberg, an award-winning black actress and his girlfriend at the time. His minstrel skit included eating watermelon. In 1997, during an interview with *New Yorker Magazine*, Goldberg defended Danson's performance and said she helped write the jokes and even coached Danson's makeup artist in the proper way to create blackface. She said their point was not to mock African Americans but rather to mock white supremacists who did not like their interracial relationship.

Twenty years later, in 2018, blackface peaked again. This time it became a flashpoint in the general American mainstream conversation when television talk show host Megyn Kelly mused on the *Today* show that she didn't understand why blackface was considered racist during Halloween. She apologized several times over the ensuing days, but her words fell flat. Within forty-eight hours, her talent agency had dropped her and another refused to represent her. She hired a lawyer and was fired by NBC after an executive told employees he did not support her comments. The fact that a popular television celebrity said she was completely unaware of the history of blackface revealed that many Americans were never taught about its influence or its lasting effect on modern mainstream customs, themes and traditions. In fact, Hollywood was one of the most iconic contributions that blackface made to American culture.

Chapter 2

The First Hollywood

In the 1800s, minstrel was Hollywood. It featured the celebrities, insiders and producers who were part of creating one of America's greatest contributions to the world stage: blackface comedy.

As part of the preeminent entertainment industry of the nineteenth century, blackface performances were marketed to the working-class population as family entertainment. It wasn't highbrow European operas but comedy skits for the masses.

Christy's Minstrels and other troupes traveled to villages and towns throughout the Northeast and found particular success in New York. They also traveled to Great Britain, where blackface was considered a popular form of quality entertainment. Minstrels performed in taverns and circuses, as well as on Broadway.

The white men who worked in these small troupes did not believe they were mocking blacks or slavery. They thought they were celebrating slaves, a sign of the times when the commodification of black labor was central to preserving the United States' growing status on the world trade route. In their minds, their work was essential to spreading the prosperity message of the New World.

Thomas Dartmouth Rice was the first person to use burnt cork makeup and pretend to be a slave named Jim Crow. Before he developed the character, he was a traveling actor who worked on frontier stages in the West and in the most popular New York theaters. He didn't become famous, though, until he took inspiration from a black man who limped. Rice said he was

Thomas D. Rice created the minstrel character Jim Crow. *Courtesy of Dance Index–Ballet Caravan, Inc.*

impressed with the man who would sing and dance as he worked in spite of his disability. Some reports claimed Rice wanted his performance to be so authentic that he purchased the man's clothes. He developed songs based on what writers described as the "peculiar dialect" of his black muse.

In 1832, Rice took the stage in Pittsburgh. He played Jim Crow as a "Kentucky cornfield Negro" in *The Rifle* by Solon Robinson. Rice danced and sang to an appreciative crowd that connected with the performance. His

Skedaddle sketch. *Courtesy of C.W. Moore, J. Crocker.*

new "Jump, Jim Crow" act soon became a nineteenth-century dance trend for those who heard it: "Wheel about, and turn about, and do jis so, Every time I wheel about, I jump Jim Crow."

His character became so popular that other actors began imitating his act. He began what today would be called a Jim Crow comedy series. He performed Jim Crow as a man who traveled around America. Some of the plays in the series included *Jim Crow Goes to Washington to Meet the President* and *Jim Crow Goes to the Foreign Service.* Like other minstrel songs, the verses and lyrics to Jim Crow's songs could change, but the dance chorus remained the same.

The Jim Crow circuit included performances in New York, Louisville, Philadelphia, Pittsburgh, Washington, D.C., Baltimore, Natchez, Charleston, Cincinnati and many small Ohio towns. Later, Rice added another character, Scipio Coon, also called Zip. Over the course of his entire career, Rice's two popular characters merged and became known simply as "Coon."

Soon, Rice took the act overseas to London and other parts of England. Later, he traveled to the United Kingdom. While there, he married. In

ZIP COON

American lithograph. ca. 1835

Minstrel character Zip Coon, who eventually became known as "Coon," in 1835. *Courtesy of Dance Index–Ballet Caravan, Inc.*

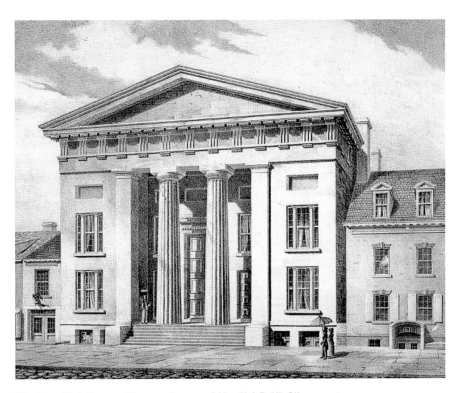

The New York Bowery Theater. *Courtesy of New York Public Library.*

1841, he returned to America as a bona fide European celebrity and created what was marketed as the first American opera. *Oh, Hush* was performed at the Bowery Theater in New York, and with it, Rice created a new industry. He was lauded as an operatic genius on the same level as the European performers. The *New York Mirror* wrote that year:

> *While the admirers of the opera flock to Park Theater to listen to the compositions of the English and Italian masters, the productions of a highly-gifted American composer should not be forgotten! The individual alluded to, although long before the public as a vocalist of extraordinary capacity, has lately attempted the difficult art of musical composition.*

The publication then goes on to compare and contrast what it calls the "Jim Crow" style to French, Scottish, Irish and Swiss operas and theaters. It notes that the new American style of opera has none of the old-world refinement. Instead, it has an atmosphere "more like nature."

While serious mainstream publications were immortalizing Rice as the leader of American theater, others immediately recognized he had committed the first American act of racial appropriation. Blackface always had strong critics who saw past the comedic musical performances. These critics were vocal for decades about the way American entertainment was normalizing mockery and stereotyping of an entire race.

One of the first was J. Kennard from New Hampshire, who wrote for the *Knickerbocker Magazine.* He penned a snarky article in response to the glowing praise of blackface theater. Kennard compares the slave to famed poet Robert Burns. Like the Scotsman, Kennard posited the slaves were from humble, untarnished backgrounds that gave them unique experiences of their country. The white American did not have this experience because he or she was essentially a transplanted European living in a "new" or "extended" Europe. Slaves, by contrast, translated and expressed America from a singular unfiltered perspective.

However, Kennard saw that slaves differed from Burns in a powerful way. Burns was nurtured and acclaimed by his society. In America, slaves were relegated to the status of a horse, so they could not be discovered or acknowledged for their creative works. For slave performance to be discovered, the white man had to steal it because the slave owners would not allow their "property" to work in theater even if they could. Kennard goes on to make the argument that slaves were the true American poets.

> *Applying this rule to America; in which class of our population must we look for our truly original and American poets? What class is secluded from foreign influences, receives the narrowest form of education, travels the shortest distance from home, has the least amount of cash to spare and mixes least with any class above itself? Our negro slaves to be sure! That is the class we should expect to find our national poets and there we do find them.*

He challenged the great poets of Europe to simply learn the language, songs, dance and culture of the American slave, just as Rice had, and perform what they saw. Once done, they, too, could add their names to the list of great American poets and performers, just like he had.

Kennard's argument made little difference. Blackface struck a chord in the masses. Soon, a series of minstrel troupes, such as the Virginia Minstrels, was working the circuits. When Christy's Minstrels arrival on the stage, they matured and transformed the industry. Christy's created a three-act play

Thomas D. Rice dressed as Jim Crow. *Courtesy of Dance Index–Ballet Caravan, Inc.*

model for minstrel skits and hired writers to create the songs. The group performed at various northern theaters, such as Niblo's Garden in New York City and other popular sites. On March 12, 1847, the *New York Tribune* stated:

> *Christy's Minstrels drawing crowded houses at the Society Library.* [Now on East Seventy-Ninth Street, at that time the Library was at Broadway and Leonard Street, in a building containing an

auditorium that was used for lectures and various theatrical events.] *Many of the most fashionable families attend, as the performances are a pleasing relief to the high toned excitement of the Italian Opera. Negro melodies are the very democracy of music.*

Christy hired his stepson George Harrington—who soon changed his name to George Christy—to compose music. Eventually, the stepson grew more famous than the elder performer. When his stepfather retired, the new troupe leader expanded the act overseas like Rice had. There, the minstrel act gained a worldwide popularity that surpassed Rice's.

Another contemporary troupe, the Bryant's Minstrels, rode the high wave of blackface popularity. The Christy and Bryant acts had the longest runs of any troupes before the Civil War, but for many decades after it, the industry had a host of celebrity blackface performers. Cool White, Joe Sweeney and Richard Ward Peel were among those who reached the popularity of George Christy.

Another Christy performer, Stephen Foster, remains one of America's most historic songwriters. For the minstrel group, he wrote "Oh! Susanna," "Old Folks at Home" and "Jeanie with the Light Brown Hair." Even today, some music historians call him the "tree trunk of American song." His

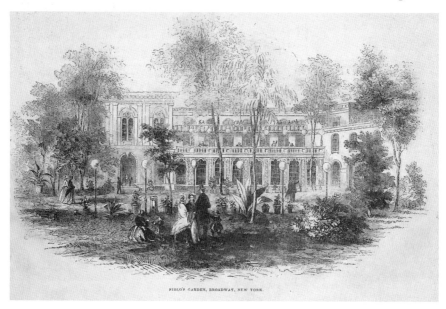

Niblo's Garden in New York City. *From* Gleason's Pictorial Drawing-Room Companion.

musical composition is studied today for its balance and emotion. He's been hailed as the composer of the "people's music." He wrote more than two hundred songs for Christy's Minstrels and other troupes. Unlike Rice, he drew influences from the Scots-Irish and the European Folk Movement rather than the African American slave business.

Other than the academic musicians who study Foster, America has largely forgotten the minstrel performers and songwriters. Their music, however, and their blackface acts had a lasting effect on the American experience. Abraham Lincoln enjoyed "Blue Tail Fly" and other syncopated minstrel tunes played on the banjo. He had an emotional connection to them. Several minstrel songs, such as "Swanee River Rock," sung by Ray Charles, would remain popular into the middle of the twentieth century. Minstrel songs wouldn't start to wane in force until rock music and MTV began to sweep the nation. "The Yellow Rose of Texas" was one of the few songs that has survived to take on an

Dance Scene from "Uncle Tom's Cabin." Niblo's Garden, New York. 1876

Courtesy of Dance Index–Ballet Caravan, Inc.

institutional life of its own. Meanwhile, Harriet Beecher Stowe's novel *Uncle Tom's Cabin*, which created a second wave of minstrel acts dubbed "Tom shows," still has a place in the American educational system.

Minstrelsy and blackface were at the forefront of Hollywood filmmaking when a leading minstrel leader in California wanted to find a way to make money off the new technology. Colonel William Selig moved minstrelsy characters and blackface onto the big screen. As the film industry transformed, minstrel characters could be portrayed with less exaggeration, although the undercurrent was still prevalent. For example, a young Shirley Temple had a famous staircase dance with Bill Robinson, known as Bojangles, in a scene from the Depression-era movie *The Little Colonel*.

Minstrel stage performances, however, would begin to lose favor in the awakening of the civil rights movement. The last attempt at a large-scale minstrel show was at the 1964 World's Fair, where the performance bombed. That does not mean that minstrel-style characters disappeared. Minstrel characters came to mass television as hit comedy shows such as

"The Great Can-Can Dance." Johnson and Powers, San Francisco Minstrels. 1878

A minstrel sketch. *Courtesy of Dance Index–Ballet Caravan, Inc.*

Leon Schottish dressed as a blackface ballerina in a Christy's Minstrels sketch. *From* Christy's Plantation Melodies.

John Diamond, a minstrel actor, in blackface. *Courtesy of Dance Index–Ballet Caravan, Inc.*

Sanford and Son, *What's Happening!* and *The Jeffersons*. These shows aired in the United States in the 1970s and 1980s.

Centuries after Rice's death, the characters he founded remain pivotal touchstones for America race relations. Jim Crow became the namesake for laws that created a nation divided on race, and Coon became an insulting reference for an African American. In that vein, a Bryant's Minstrel performer, Dan Emmett, wrote a song that has embedded itself into America's culture with a gravitas that well surpasses Christy's "Yellow Rose of Texas." Emmett was known for his grand walk-around finales that distinguished themselves from Rice's trademark of mimicking slave songs. Emmett used direct elements of slave songs, but he used the white American "old-fashioned" fiddle for instrumentation.

One of these "hybrid songs" was called "Dixie Land." Over the course of Emmett's career, he rewrote the song for different performances, and it became known as "Dixie." His last rewrite would become an anthem for Confederate America.

Chapter 3

Five Points

Juba jump and Juba sing
Juba cut dat pigeon's wing
Juba kick off Juba's shoe
Juba dance dat Jubal Jew

Juba whirl dat foot about
Juba blow dat candle out
Juba circle, raise de latch
Juba do dat Long Dog Scratch

As minstrelsy continued its rise to worldwide acceptance, the industry opened its doors to black actors in the late 1830s. These black actors would perform one of two portrayals of people of color. The actors had a choice between Jim Crow, the fanciful plantation slave who danced and sang his way through his bad fortune, or the Jim Dandy, the fancy northern free black who wore expensive clothes and had an air of high affluence. The most popular of these black minstrel actors was known as Masta Juba, and he was a worldwide sensation.

William Henry Lane was born a free person of color in New York City circa 1825. He had little family influence and lived in Five Points, an entrenched slum. Filled with immigrants, free people of color and slaves from throughout the world, it was the original American melting pot. He was not unlike many children who were born in Five Points. He basically

William Lane dressed as Masta Juba for a minstrel skit. *Courtesy of Dance Index–Ballet Caravan, Inc.*

was left to raise himself in a world that was filled with debauchery. Children raised in Five Points grew up fast. Race was not a factor in this scenario.

Christian missionaries who were determined to clean up Five Points described a typical dysfunctional family scene that left the boys headed for jail. They described mothers who drank all day and girls who were hardened when they shouldn't have been.

> *Men are there—whose only occupation is thieving, and sensuality in every form, of every grade, and who know of no restraint, except the fear of the strong police, who hover continually about these precincts. And boys are there by scores, so fearfully mature in all that is vicious and degrading, that soon, O how soon, they will be fit only for the prison and the gallows.*

Ironically, the slums began within a one-minute walk east of city hall and its swanky, clean, upscale neighborhood. Five Points was not a place most people wanted to remain. It was at the crossroads of Little-Water, Cross, Anthony, Orange and Mulberry. The missionaries described this intersection as the streets that entered the slum like "rivers emptying themselves into a bay." In the center was Paradise Square, where the residents would hand their garments to dry on a wooden piling that surrounded it. The Old Brewery, a building made popular by a song and story about it, was opposite the park.

The neighborhood was filled with brawls, fights, peddlers and beggars. Livestock roamed in the streets alongside entertainment and lodging. Grocery stores sold more liquor than food. Substandard housing was built

FIVE POINTS, 1827.

A satirical painting of Five Points highlighting the district's renowned chaos and vulgarity. *Courtesy of the Metropolitan Museum of Art.*

The Old Brewery in Five Points, circa 1820. *Courtesy of* The Old Brewery and the New Mission House at the Five Points *in the public domain.*

around Fresh Pond, a protected watering hole that the city regulated to ensure fish remained in it. The missionaries described the neighborhood: "Miserable-looking buildings, liquor-stores innumerable, neglected children by scores, playing in rags and dirt, squalid-looking women, brutal men with black eyes and disfigured faces, proclaiming drunken brawls and fearful violence, complete the general picture."

It was a hard place, with people who were all hoping to find the prosperity, or at least the safety, that the New World promised. It was a broken promise for most, according to the missionaries.

> *Gaze on it, ye men of business and of wealth, and calculate anew the amount of taxation for police restraints and support, made necessary by the existence of a place like this. And gaze on it Christian men, with tearful eyes—tears of regret and shame—that long ere now the Christian Church has not combined its moral influences, and tested their utmost strength to purge a place so foul; for this, reader, is the "Five Points!"*

Lane was like other free blacks of his hometown. Not much was known about how he gained his status since slaves were certainly part of the

45

neighborhood. In fact, in 1741, when the slum was being developed, thirteen slaves were burned at the stake amid a run of robberies and thefts that were blamed on "the negro." At the time, New York had twelve thousand residents, and one-sixth of that number were slaves. The burnings occurred at the intersection of Pearl and Chatham Streets. Another twenty slaves were hanged—one in iron chains—on a nearby island in Fresh Pond. The thirty-three deaths did not clean up the neighborhood, and it would remain the armpit of New York City for centuries to come. To be born in Five Points was considered a life sentence of unforgiving poverty regardless of a person's race, gender or age, according to the missionaries. The missionaries knew that life in Five Points was hard and wrote:

> *What does that name import? It is the synonym for ignorance the most entire, for misery the most abject, for crime of the darkest dye, for degradation so deep that human nature cannot sink below it. We hear it, and visions of sorrow—of irremediable misery—flit be-fore our mental vision. Infancy and childhood, without a mother's care or a father's protection: born in sin, nurtured in crime; the young mind sullied in its first bloom, the young heart crushed before its tiny call for affection has met one answering response.*

It was in this poverty environment that Lane developed a gift for dance. He most likely learned the skill from Uncle Jim Lowe, a black man who danced in the neighborhood. The elder earned his money in the saloons, dance halls and theaters in and around Five Points.

As Lane learned slave dances from Uncle Jim, he also picked up a series of tricks and techniques from the traditional dances that the Europeans knew. The diversity of this sordid squalor meant Lane was also exposed to Irish jigs and other old-world styles. Lane was a unique dancer because he had an ability to combine slave and European cultures into a distinctive style that probably made him one of the first "crossover" performers in the entertainment world.

By the time Lane was fifteen years old, he was completely without family. When the minstrels learned about him, they adopted him into their fraternal bonds and gave him a home. They recognized his genius ability to execute a graceful combination of black slave dance with European influences. Like other minstrels, he had a stage name. Lane became "Masta Juba." The title reflected a name given to an entertaining slave. Most slaves renamed "Juba" were accomplished in slave song, instruments or dance. Lane danced to a song by the name, which, like "The Yellow Rose of Texas," became a pop culture hit. People would sing it while they tried to dance like him. The *New York Herald* described one of his performances in Five Points:

> *At the time when he performed at Pete Williams', in Orange Street, New York, those who passed through the long hallway and entered the dance hall, after paying their shilling to the darky doorkeeper, whose "box-office" was a plain soap box, or a wooden one of that description, saw this phenomenon, "Juba," imitate all the dancers of the day and their special steps. Then Bob Ellingham, the interlocutor and master of ceremonies, would say, "Now, Master Juba, show your own jig." Whereupon he would go through all his own steps and specialties, with never a resemblance in any of them to those he had just imitated.*

Lane joined the Pell's Ethiopian Serenaders, where he became known as the most famous dancer in the world. Dance became his ticket out of Five Points, and he performed with the Ethiopian minstrels until he went on tour in England. After that, he never returned to Five Points or America. He died in 1852 on tour. Lane, a free man of color who assumed a slave name to dance in front of white audiences, was left to obscurity after his death until renewed interest in him would awaken almost two hundred years later. Today, a resurgence of research on his life has begun as serious music historians recognize him as the early founder of one of the New World's most influential art forms: the American tap dance.

By the 1830s, Lane was already popular as the minstrel character Masta Juba when a New Haven woman named Emily D. West walked into Five Points trying to escape the violence facing people of color in Connecticut. She came with a few of her neighbors who were also seeking respite from the race issues. Throughout the North, free people of color were far fewer in number than European white immigrants, but they were larger in number than slaves. West arrived in New York as a single woman with her free papers and the hope of finding a new life away from the riots that were plaguing New Haven. When she arrived, however, she found life harsher and harder than the one she was trying to escape.

Five Points was the embodiment of the second-class status for anyone who had the misfortune of living there. For free blacks, it was their only option. This wasn't the case in New Haven. In Connecticut, several established neighborhoods—even if they were collections of substandard homes—existed for free blacks throughout the urban centers. In New York, free blacks competed with other poor white immigrants, such as the

Pell's Ethiopian Serenaders. ca. 1848

Juba jump and Juba sing
Juba cut dat pigeon's wing
Juba kick off Juba's shoe
Juba dance dat Jubal Jew

Juba whirl dat foot about
Juba blow dat candle out
Juba circle, raise de latch
Juba do dat Long Dog Scratch.

(Juba-song in William Handy's *Blues*)

The Pell's Ethiopean Serenaders playbook cover features Masta Juba, an African American from Five Points in New York who became the most famous minstrel dancer of his time. *Courtesy of Dance Index–Ballet Caravan, Inc.*

Irish, for resources, jobs and living quarters. In Connecticut, Emily lived near Yale College, which was the heartbeat for the new progressive race thinkers of the day.

In fact, while Lane maneuvered his way through slum bars and saloons, leading abolitionists supported Emily and her friends. When their lives collided in Five Points, both experienced institutionalized racism but from very different perspectives. One common experience, however, was their freedom papers. These documents were the tickets from slavery. Free blacks always carried them on their bodies. Slaves were still sold on the auction block during Emily's years in Connecticut, which meant she constantly had to prove she wasn't a slave. Auctions continued in New Haven until 1825. In New York, meanwhile, free blacks were routinely kidnapped, sold into slavery and shipped to southern plantations.

Lane never saw the southern plantations where more slaves than free blacks worked the economy. Emily and her friends would see that land. It was called Tejas, and the Mexican-occupied land was being called the New South. Tejas wouldn't be a slum, but it would be a place of war beyond any social fight she ever experienced. Tejas, or Texas, would be a land that would change her life. It would also be a land that would mark her as its own for centuries after she left it. Emily D. West would be long gone before she would become the Yellow Rose of Texas.

Chapter 4

A Product of the Times

Emily D. West wasn't a dancer, singer or entertainer like Lane, although, like him, she was a common middle-class free black who was a product of the times. She was born in New Haven, Connecticut, in 1801, after the Gradual Abolition Act began sweeping the North, first in Pennsylvania and then in Massachusetts and New Hampshire. Connecticut followed the trend. The act, passed in Philadelphia, made it illegal for slave owners to take a pregnant slave into a slave state so her child could be born into slavery. Essentially, the law ensured that all black children born after 1784 would become free people of color when they became adults. Also, the child would be registered as a citizen within six months after birth. In Connecticut, the law originally stated that a child would gain his or her freedom at the age of twenty-five. In 1797, the age was lowered to twenty-one.

It could have been possible that Emily had a father who was already a free person of color. In 1776, the state allowed blacks who fought in the Revolutionary War to gain their status as free people of color. Between three hundred and four hundred men agreed to gain their citizenship rights through military service. Also, if her mother was a free black woman at the time of her birth, she would have inherited that status. However, the name of her mother is unknown, and the last name West was popular for free blacks in New Haven at the time. Nothing more is known about Emily's parents. Nothing has been found that documents she was biracial or, as it was described then, mulatto. It remains unknown

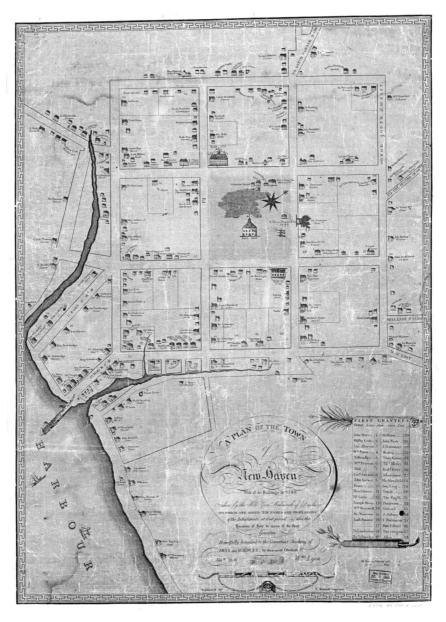

A map of New Haven as it would have appeared near the time of Emily D. West's birth.
Courtesy of Library of Congress.

if her father was another race. Some recent historians have suggested her parents could have been a free black couple who lived in New Haven in 1823. Regardless, Emily was born at a time when her freedom would have been assured by birth or by law.

As the *post nati* law began to take effect, New Haven saw a rise in free blacks and a decline in the slave population. In 1800, almost 5 percent of the population was black. Of that number, 166 were free and 82 were slaves. Ten years later, the number of free blacks had more than doubled, to 377, and only 18 slaves remained. However, while free blacks had rights not granted to slaves, they were still denied access to white schools and were not allowed to vote. Also, slavery did not end neatly in the North, so free blacks always had to have their "papers" on them to prove their status. Emily was no different. The complicated relationship the government had with slavery also meant that many families that were free still had relatives or family who were slaves. Manumission was ad hoc and at the will of the slave owner, so while some free black families might live around Long Island Sound, they might still be visiting or having contact with slaves. This meant Emily lived during a time when racial tensions would percolate into deep divisions. During her young years, New Haven saw an increase in self-made free black men, like William Lanson, who was an engineer, developer and contractor. Between 1810 and 1812, he extended New Haven's wharf into deep water, which set the stage for it to become a wealthy seaport. His endeavor came after several attempts by the government and the commercial sector to build a unified wharf system.

Several other white men tried to complete the project in various stages but never could. When Lanson finished, the wharf was three-quarters of a mile long, making it the longest pier in the country at the time. He was also instrumental in the development of free black neighborhoods that provided homes for the emerging black population far from Whitting Street, where white families were. Emily would have lived in one of these neighborhoods.

Free blacks lived in the factory district east of Long Island Sound and southeast of New Haven. This community was southeast of Yale College and the fashionable New Haven Green with its stately two-story homes. Houses around Long Island Sound were less grand. That neighborhood was dubbed "Poverty Square" by 1830. Most of the homes were shacks. Some families lived in underground cellars that were poorly constructed. Lanson would reconstruct old barns to create new dwellings for free blacks and Irish families who were also discriminated against by the establishment. The dwellings become known as New Liberia and New Guinea, where free blacks

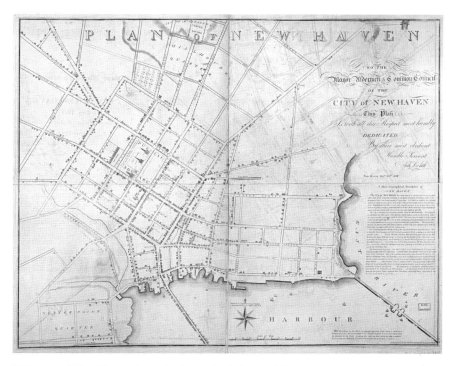

This map of New Haven shows the long wharf. *Courtesy of Library of Congress.*

lived as a community. In New Liberia, a sort of liberal attitude emerged that irritated pious New Englanders. At one point, Lanson reconstructed a slaughterhouse into the Liberian Hotel. It was created as room and board for indigents, sailors and railroad workers. Interracial couples were welcomed. The hotel gained a reputation as a party atmosphere that included a copious amount of rotgut, a potentially deadly form of bad liquor, and corn whiskey. When a mob ensued in 1831, the police only arrested the whites who were there because they weren't concerned with the blacks' "morals." New Liberia maintained its reputation as "a vice-center" until it burned down in 1845.

New Guinea, however, became the neighborhood that free blacks moved to as they became more prosperous. This neighborhood was closer to Yale College and near a manicured New Haven town square. It was a relief from the squalor, crime and vice raids of New Liberia. Negro Lane was the main drag. The name was later changed to State Street. The lane ran northeast from the town square to a commercial/agriculture center along the Connecticut River. While it was a nicer neighborhood, the land was still difficult to cultivate and suffered from poor drainage.

Since West was a common surname for free blacks in New Haven at the time, it is possible that Emily's family was from one of the segregated neighborhoods that began to rise in New Haven. Sodom Hill was situated near West Creek, where many free blacks would process cattle and hides for export to Jamaica plantations. The British had built a vast plantation economy in Jamaica during the last part of the 1700s. They imported slaves from several areas of Africa, but most were from the Bight of Biafra, which is known today as the Bight of Bonny, near Cameroon. These slave traders mainly brought women and children and by 1780 had a surplus of slaves landing on the Caribbean shores. This prompted the slave traders to begin a re-export campaign that brought slaves to the New World and other countries. Therefore, Jamaica was a prosperous port for the North to do business with. Residents from Sodom lived on a rise of West Creek that descended into a marsh that surrounded it. The neighborhood was the most polluted area of New Haven and in the 1800s had an unsavory reputation. The marsh separated it from the city, and the high ground along Columbus Avenue was the heart of the neighborhood. Tanneries left carcasses lying around, which created

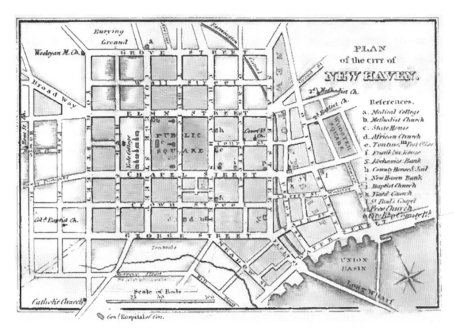

This map of New Haven shows major landmarks around the public square in the 1800s. *Courtesy of Library of Congress.*

byproducts. Raw sewage drained into the creek. Disease was rampant. The death rate was higher than among the white population in New Haven where residents had better healthcare access. Most free blacks from Sodom Hill worked in Trowbridge Square doing menial work. Women from Sodom Hill would work as domestic servants such as nursery workers, governesses, maids, laundry washers and dressmakers.

Despite the institutional urban discrimination, free blacks made progress. The neighborhoods had signs of a rising middle and upper class. Lanson amassed $40,000 during his lifetime and gained the title "King Lanson" or "Lanson, the African King." By 1854, Reverend A.G. Beamon, the pastor of the Temple Street Congregational Church, reported that New Haven had two thousand free blacks who owned $200,000 worth of real estate, banks and railroad stocks. They worshiped at four Methodist churches, one Congregational church, one Episcopal church and one Baptist church. A literary society maintained a library. Four schools taught children. That didn't mean, however, that this progress was welcomed. A segment of the white community was jealous of King Lanson and the two thousand free blacks who were part of the rising class.

Chapter 5

Colonists versus Militants

King Lanson didn't retain his title or his money. When he began to amass wealth, build neighborhoods and try to provide affordable housing for blacks, he started to attract criticism from the white community. The Liberian Hotel was a main source of distraction for him, and over time, he was held responsible for the actions of his tenants. He claimed to have been in jail over four hundred times. The repeated arrests began to systematically dismantle his wealth and legacy. He died penniless in an almshouse. His obituary was scathing and called him a man of low morals and repute even though it also heralded his brilliance. To maintain his reputation, he penned his autobiography, but like Emily, he left no details about his birth or early years. It's not clear if he was born in New Haven as a free black or if he escaped slavery. He focused his life in his own terms. He discussed success in New Haven and the discrimination that occurred after he began using his wealth to build a black community and other similar communities for marginalized groups.

When Lanson was building the neighborhoods where Emily lived, the white establishment had begun shifting its attitude about slavery and abolition. In 1816, the American Colonization Society organized. The white society was dedicated to creating a new black country in Africa so that when slavery ended, blacks could be sent there to live. They succeeded to some extent, and Liberia in Africa was created to recolonize slaves. In the beginning, the American Colonization Society was a home for abolitionists, many of whom supported Lanson and wanted to see him succeed. But

Portrait of Author Tappan. *From* Life of Arthur Tappan.

over time, the society began to fracture over whether blacks should be sent to Africa or be allowed to live in an equal America. Emily would eventually align herself with the latter, and the decision would set her on a path to Texas.

Prominent abolitionist Lewis Tappan remembered the fracture and said it happened when it became obvious that the "colonists" were not abolitionists under the same definition that he and his brother, Arthur, considered themselves. Colonists, he said, were really seeking to rid America of all blacks. He said they wanted to see slaves and free people of color like Emily relocate to Africa. "The society had its origin, and main support in prejudice against color; this caste feeling was strengthened by it; sending to Africa ignorant slaves, emancipated for the special purpose, and a degraded portion of the free people of color, did not tend to the civilization and elevation of themselves, or the people of that country."

The Tappan brothers and their supporters left the society. They were dubbed the "militant abolitionists." Simeon Smith Jocelyn was among this group. He was a noted engraver in New Haven who built schools for young children in Emily's neighborhood and pastored the old Temple Street church that welcomed whites and blacks. Both races worshiped unsegregated. He also had a vision and led the charge for the first black college in America and worked for years to see it come to a vote at the New Haven City Council one fateful night.

JOCELYN'S NEW HAVEN PROGRAMS

Jocelyn, William Grayson and Arthur Tappan were the leaders of the New Haven abolitionists. In 1830, they organized themselves with free blacks at a convention in Philadelphia. In the minutes of that convention, the following are their reasons for locating the proposed college in New Haven:

1. The site is healthy and beautiful.
2. Its inhabitants are friendly, pious, generous and humane.
3. Its laws are salutary and protecting to all, without regard to complexion, etc., etc.

Jocelyn was about the same age as Emily and knew her. He was born to an educated and progressive family in 1797 and raised on the north side of Long Island Sound. He studied at Yale under Dr. Nathaniel Taylor and was ordained a minister in 1829. Taylor was the founder of a fierce and emotional doctrine called "The New Haven Theology." While Jocelyn studied, he attended Taylor's Center Church with other abolitionists like Eli Whitney. He also had a friendship with Noah and Nathanial Webster. Taylor had a beautiful church with a large steeple, and he led a segregated congregation. Whites were on the first floor; blacks and Indians were on the second. From their high overlook, the Indians and blacks were expressive in their responses to the pastor, which made whites describe them as "unruly." However, in 1824, Jocelyn opened Temple Church, where blacks and whites were equal. They sat together in worship, and no one was considered "unruly." The church was a plain wooden building with no great architectural details. The nonplastered structure was thirty by forty feet. One hundred people worshiped there each Sunday. Emily probably worshiped there and was part of Jocelyn's work.

The approach that Jocelyn had toward opening charities, societies, developments and other programs began to raise the status and opportunities for the free black middle class in New Haven. After Jocelyn opened the church, he created the African Ecclesiastical Society, which included black committee members and segments of his congregation. Four years later, Temple Church became a Congregational church in the United African Society. This officially made it the nation's first black Congregational church. The congregation consisted of four men and seventeen women. The following year, he opened the first school for black children, a Sunday school known as the African Sabbath School. It had a day school for children and a night school for adults. Emily might have attended classes here, but it was more likely that she learned to read and write at one of the free black community schools for children that began in 1811. In 1824, the community began a six-term school. It's possible that she worked in them.

Jocelyn's programs began to create division while his friends antagonized the establishment with their impatience to see an equal America. To push the immediate emancipation of slaves, abolitionist William Lloyd Garrison

YALE COLLEGE.

As a free black woman, Emily D. West lived among abolitionists associated with Yale University. *From* History of Antiquities of New Haven, Conn.

5. View of NEW HAVEN and FORT HALE.
a. West Rock. b. Long Wharf. c. Pavilion Gymnasium. d. Steam boat Office. e. East Rock. g. Tomlinson's bridge. h. Fort Hale.

New Haven was the birthplace of Emily D. West. *From* History of Antiquities of New Haven, Conn.

denounced the United States Constitution at one point. He made the incredible statement because he thought western expansion was a bad bargain designed to keep America unified. At that time, the North and South agreed to allow slavery in the new territories.

Jocelyn, meanwhile, thought New Haven could become the United States headquarters of abolition. He wanted New Haven to be a welcoming spot for all free blacks to immigrate to from all over the world, especially Jamaica. He envisioned a great relationship between New Haven and Yale College. He had no idea at the time that the violent backlash to his vision would drive Emily out of New Haven with him.

THE STORY OF GENERAL NAT

A bloody slave revolt about five hundred miles away in Southampton, Virginia, made headlines in New Haven newspapers in August 1831. Jocelyn and his friends were considered militants for their great fiery rhetoric against American race politics, but they were lightweights compared to Nat Turner. Turner was a black minister who had been dubbed "General Nat," and he conducted a militant rebellion across the state. Under his leadership, fifty slaves killed white families and staged revolts that sent a strong message. Turner had no time for politics. He was prepared to lead bloody rebellions until he saw the emancipation of slaves. One of his strategic maneuvers was to capture the town of Jerusalem on the Nottoway River. For this, Jerusalem did not nail him to the cross. Instead, the Virginia militia cut off the slaves' heads. They captured Turner and hanged his body from a tree. After he hung for a few days, Jerusalem did not lay his body in a tomb. The townspeople dismembered it and decapitated it. Then they dissected and skinned it. The gruesome retaliation did not end there. His skin was tanned and sold as souvenirs. After the episode was over, slaves throughout Virginia plantations were filled with fear.

In New Haven, the white community—as liberal and progressive as it was—was also filled with a reverberating fear of slave uprisings. The establishment wanted to stop new black immigrations. Those in charge did not want their town to be a destination for free black education or work.

The South's interpretation of General Nat's rebellion did not cast blame on the plantation economy and its use of slave labor. The South blamed the northern abolitionists and their movement to bring equality to America and end slavery. To further stoke the fears of the white population, the rebellion came on the heels of the Haitian Riot, in which white plantation owners were killed. It was among the bloodiest rebellions at the time and compounded fears that blacks would rise against whites in a race war. Between General Nat and the Haitian Riot, New Haven and the rest of the United States had a rising fear of free blacks and slaves.

THE TALE OF THE FREE BLACK COLLEGE

It was only one month after General Nat's rebellion, on September 10, 1831, that New Haven City Council met to discuss the opening of a free black college. A local newspaper, which was not against the measure, reported that Jocelyn was the only person who continued to actively push the agenda after the rebellions. The newspaper wrote:

> *It will be seen by an advertisement in this paper, that a call is made on our citizens, to meet this day, and express their opinion on the expediency of establishing a College, in this city, for the education of colored persons. We do not know, but we are slow of heart to believe, but we confess we cannot think there are just grounds to fear the establishment of any such institution in this town.*

Arthur Tappan purchased the land and offered $1,000 toward the $20,000 needed to build the college. The newspaper also claimed he was the only person who wanted to fund it. With that, the editors said the school should be built in a neighboring town.

> *Notwithstanding all the idle reports, we do not believe that money can be raised for such a purpose to make it worthwhile for any man or body of men to spend time in talking in favor or against such an institution. Besides, who would think of locating a School or College in a town where forty-nine-fiftieths of the inhabitants are against the project?*

The New Haven mayor and aldermen had a heated town meeting that did not go well. Lewis Tappan remembered the incident. His brother was in New York and could not attend:

There was great excitement. Mr. Jocelyn calmly stated the facts and corrected some of the many misrepresentations. But very few of those supposed to be favorable to the enterprise, came forward in this exigency to sustain it.... The opposers of the measure rallied in strong force and were vociferous in opposition.

The council voted to deny a free black college because "it was auxiliary to the agitation against the municipal institution of slavery and incompatible with the prosperity, if not the existence of Yale college." A steady stream of wealthy southern students attended Yale, and administrators feared a nearby black college would affect enrollment. At the town meeting, only five men voted for it: Jocelyn, his brother and three others. The unexpected hostility Jocelyn received surprised him, and he abandoned the measure forever.

His support for whites who wanted to teach blacks to read and write also caused criticism to rise against him. Later in the year, Jocelyn and Arthur Tappan sympathized with Prudence Crandall, a Quaker woman who wanted to allow free black girls to attend her young ladies' academy. The effort resulted in fierce opposition. It took two years, but eventually the Connecticut legislature retaliated with the "Black Law." As a result of the 1833 legislation, Crandall's school was destroyed and her home damaged. She fled to Illinois for safety.

In response to the continued opposition and unrest, Jocelyn's comrades combined three antislavery forces under one umbrella. The New York Anti-Slavery Society and the New England Anti-Slavery Society joined with the Society of Friends—a Quaker organization—to become the American Anti-Slavery Society. As these efforts continued, proslavery riots began to sweep New England and Connecticut. Anger toward abolitionists grew. Connecticut passed laws to stop black schools from opening. More measures were used to strip away free black rights.

A year later, in 1834, Jocelyn's home was attacked by a mob while he was there. Emily might have been a member of the household when the incident happened. Regardless, she had to have known about it. The attack rattled Jocelyn so much that he sent out a national call to the abolitionist network that New Haven was not safe anymore.

He relocated to New York. Emily did too. Other New Haven free blacks who also moved there included Diane Leonard, George Copper, a thirteen-year-old free black and a biracial boy named Turner. They probably lived with Emily when they all arrived. Jocelyn might have even traveled with them and paid their fare. When Emily arrived, she would know the squalor of Five Points. She would, however, have also seen free black women acting as entrepreneurs. New York's lower Manhattan was home to fourteen thousand free blacks when Emily lived there.

Once Jocelyn arrived, he met with Joshua Levitt and the Tappan brothers. They reimagined Jocelyn's vision for New Haven and found ways to dovetail it with the Tappan brothers' efforts to raise the quality of life for the free blacks of New York. Jocelyn thought he had found hostility in New Haven, but within months of that meeting, he would learn it was nothing compared to New York.

And it would all erupt at a blackface minstrel theater where Masta Juba danced.

Chapter 6

The Webb of Fake News

Emily, Jocelyn and the rest of their group landed in New York when it was an active volcano. The big city was chaos. Competition between the different races and ethnic groups was a world different from New Haven. The social issues were so difficult to address that southerners would use Five Points as an example of how much worse life would be for blacks if slavery didn't exist. Community sentiment against free blacks was much higher than in Connecticut. It had been eighty-seven years since New York had erupted in riots, but that was about to change.

When Jocelyn and Emily arrived with their group, Arthur Tappan was delighted that his trusted colleague was with him, and according to Lewis Tappan, they approached their work as a ministry.

> It was during the year 1834 and afterward that Mr. Tappan, accompanied by his long tried and devoted friend Mr. Jocelyn, who had moved to New York, was accustomed on Sabbath mornings to explore the streets in the ward where the poor people of color chiefly dwelt, visit them in their different rooms, inquire into their wants, administer relief, give them useful advice, invite them to Sabbathschools, often praying with them.

Free blacks were maligned and discriminated against in New York communities. At church, they were no longer allowed to associate with white parishioners during service; they sat in the back. Free blacks were given communion after the whites and were excluded from social and educational activities. They were refused seats on omnibuses and had to ride at the back of steamers.

One of the first endeavors Jocelyn helped Tappan create was the educational arm of the Phoenix Society, an organization of young free blacks. The brainchild was an extension of Jocelyn's quashed plans in New Haven. Samuel Cornish, a Presbyterian minister and the publisher of the first black newspaper in the nation, was the manager. Tappan paid his salary and the administrative costs. An interracial board of directors ran the society. Cornish was also known as the leader of the free black community in New York and a member of the American Anti-Slavery Society.

The Phoenix Society was committed to registering free blacks and recording their existence in New York. It also attempted to create a master job bank. The bank, or list, recorded who had what skills and mechanical ability so the board could help free blacks get jobs. Membership required a quarterly donation. Emily might have been involved with at least one of the society's programs. Free black women were encouraged to organize into their own societies and begin clothing drives for students who agreed to attend school. She might have also helped Jocelyn organize lyceums, or education events, so lifelong learning could become embedded in the community. The society also stressed the importance of church attendance and learning good manners, such as punctuality. Jocelyn described his joy that the Phoenix Society's lyceums soon extended its branches to Philadelphia and Boston and were fanning his hopes of a black college. Lewis Tappan recalled:

> *These meetings were rather social, but compositions, essays, poetry, etc., were read by the authors, (young women as well as young men attending,) and topics of interest were discussed in a familiar way. The refreshments were very simple—a cracker and a glass of water—thus avoiding costly preparations of refreshment, which are adverse to mental improvement.…It was natural that these attentions to the moral and intellectual wants of the colored people should have suggested the idea of a high school, or college, particularly as colored youth were excluded from them throughout the country.*

In the spring of 1834, Jocelyn's organization agitated the community, but the residents weren't angry until Arthur Tappan, the man with the money, sat next to Cornish at the Laight Street Church, where Samuel Cox was the pastor. The rich man's decision riled the colonization movement. The seeds for the abolitionist movement were watered in that one act and caught the attention of the media.

Portrait of James Webb. *From Life of Arthur Tappan.*

James Watson Webb, publisher of the *New York Courier and Enquirer*, was an anti-abolitionist, and he began to increase stories about Jocelyn and the Tappan brothers' works. He wrote stories that the society encouraged white women to marry blacks. To illustrate the point, Webb published articles that said black dandies (one of the caricatures portrayed in the minstrel acts) were riding horses along Broadway in order to find white women to marry. He also wrote that the church pastor, Samuel Cox, said God was black. Finally, he wrote articles that said Arthur Tappan left his white wife to marry a black woman. By the summer, tempers erupted.

On July 7, a black congregation received permission to use another white Presbyterian church, the Chatham Street Chapel. They wanted to conduct a celebration for New York's emancipation of slaves. The congregation was supposed to use the church on the Fourth of July, but the celebration was rescheduled when white spectators began harassing them. The New York Sacred Music Society usually had meetings on the night of the emancipation celebration, but it had canceled. Because of that, church leaders allowed the black congregation to use it. Hughes, a free black orator, was about to read the Declaration of Independence when the music society leader, Dr. Rockwell, walked by with Justice Lowndes, a police officer. Rockwell was incensed to see that free blacks were in the pews on a night his organization normally used the church. He was unaware of the rescheduling. He told other members of the society, and they went inside the church to demand that the free blacks leave. When the free blacks refused, Rockwell and other society members began to forcibly remove them. Chairs and lamps were thrown. Loaded canes were used to beat the crowd. The free blacks fought back and overpowered them.

News of the fight spread through town, and soon other people arrived to join the fracas. Eventually, the police were called. Officers arrested six free blacks and locked the church. However, the fight kept on in the street. It ended when the free blacks were outnumbered. As it ended, some whites noticed Lewis Tappan was among the crowd. They followed him and taunted him with hoots and yells. When he arrived home, they threw stones at his house.

Webb reported in his paper the next day that the incident was an infringement on white rights and then squarely placed blame for the entire incident on Arthur Tappan and his abolitionist efforts, according to his brother. Webb's report that day stated:

> *The riot at the chapel last evening was a riot commenced and carried on by the negroes themselves. The white citizens present were there with no disposition to disturb the blacks. It was the Sacred Music Society alone that interfered, as they were fully justified in doing: and when they mildly insisted on their clear rights they were beaten—yes, beaten, fellow-citizens, by the bludgeons of an infuriated and an encouraged negro mob! How much longer are we to submit? In the name of the country, in the name of heaven, how much more are we to hear from Arthur Tappan's mad impertinence?*

By comparison, the *New York Evening Post* issued a critical response to Webb's account. The editors aligned with Lewis Tappan's insider knowledge. That article stated: "The story is told in the morning journals, in very inflammatory language, and the whole blame is cast upon the negroes; yet it seems to us, from those very statements themselves, that, as usual, there have been faults on both sides, and more especially on the side of the whites."

The *Post* article didn't concern Webb, and the next day, he printed a new story that said he'd become aware the Chatham Street Chapel was going to host an abolitionist meeting. Lewis Tappan charged that the story was a bold lie. A meeting was never organized, he claimed. An emboldened Webb reported in his publication:

> *Learning that there is to be another meeting tonight at Chatham-street chapel, we caution the colored people of this city against it. No one who saw the temper which pervaded last night can doubt that if the blacks continue to allow themselves to be made the tools of a few blind zealots, the consequences to them will be most serious.*

Then, the next day, Webb published an entirely fabricated account of the meeting that never happened, according to Lewis Tappan. Tappan remembered: "The paper states that a considerable crowd collected in front of the entrance to the chapel, (the gates of which were closed,) and remained for some time in silence, as if waiting to learn the result."

Then, Tappan referenced Webb's account of the meeting that did not occur:

> *"No indications of a meeting, however, were apparent," said the editor; but, in the same paper, he afterwards said, "it seems that a meeting was held; the mayor appeared accompanied by the district attorney and some police officers, and the meeting hastily adjourned." The only meeting held, it is believed, was that of the rioters, who were in search of the law-abiding abolitionists, and the peaceable people of color.*

An echo chamber started around Webb's report as people repeated it. It soon took on a life of its own. More New York papers began to report that the city's free blacks were going to set the city ablaze. Webb's report spurred several thousand white New Yorkers, who arrived at the church a second time. The mayor of New York, George Hall, tried to calm the rioters at the church, but when they erupted with three cheers for Webb, Hall was pushed aside. The rioters marched to Lewis Tappan's home, threw the family furniture out of the windows and then burned it all in the street. Arthur Tappan, who financed the church's construction, was ridiculed.

At the church, rioters had hoped to find abolitionists in a meeting. When they didn't, they began a "counter meeting." They conducted the meeting in a mocking black dialect and called for the deportation of all blacks to Africa. William Wilder was called to the podium, where he gave a speech about the horrors of sudden emancipation as he told the crowd about his experience during the Saint Domingo slave rebellion. Wilder said the group should close the meeting and regroup when the abolitionists had their next meeting. The group didn't listen to him.

The rioters decided to head for the Bowery Theater, where George P. Farren was being honored at his own blackface theater with the play *Metamora*. It was one of the most popular Jacksonian-era plays about Indians. J.T. Headly, who attended the meeting, remembered how the mob formed:

> *At all events, the mob resolved on the latter course, and streaming up the Bowery in one wild, excited mass, gathered with loud shouts in front of the theatre. The doors were closed in their faces, but pressing against them with their immense weight, they gave way, and like a dark, stormy wave, they surged up the aisles toward the footlights. In the garish light, faces grew pale, and turned eagerly toward the doors for a way of escape.*

Farren became the whipping boy for the frustrations of New Yorkers against the British, whose abolitionist movement inspired the American one, Headly wrote. Farren had been accused of slurring Americans and firing an American actor. That was enough to make him a target. Headly reported that the English supported Jocelyn's friend the irascible William Lloyd Garrison, who had denounced the U.S. Constitution, and this enraged the mob.

> *The attacks on us by the English, for upholding slavery, and their sympathy and aid for* [William] *Garrison, and co-operation with him in agitating the question of abolition in this country, had rekindled the old slumbering feeling of hostility to that country; and Mr. Farren, the stage manager of the Bowery, being an Englishman, it was transferred to him.*

The mob grew to four thousand rioters. They broke through the Bowery doors when Edwin Forrest was performing the play. The minstrel actor was at the height of his popularity and a definite New York favorite, but he could not calm them. The mayor attempted to do so but was rebuked. The mob calmed when George Washington Dixon performed as Zip Coon and then did a skit as Yankee Doodle. After that, the police showed up with billy clubs and drove them out. Farren hid during the entire episode.

Once the crowd had gathered in the street, someone began ringing a bell and shouted that they should head to Lewis Tappan's home. Headley remembered the night.

> *But instead of going to his house, they went to that of his brother, Lewis, in Rose Street, a still more obnoxious Abolitionist. Reaching it, they staved open the doors, and smashed in the windows, and began to pitch the furniture into the street. Chairs, sofas, table, pictures, mirrors, and bedding, went out one after another. But all at once a lull occurred in the work of destruction. In pitching the pictures out, one came across a portrait of Washington. Suddenly the cry arose, "It is…Washington! For God's sake, don't burn Washington!"*

Arthur Tappan heard about his brother's home and disguised himself so he could blend in with the crowd. Once he saw the destruction, he and Jocelyn went to the mayor. They asked him to send the police to stop the mob, which he did.

After tearing down white people's homes, the rioters began a violent spree in Five Points. Blacks were tortured, robbed and raped. Rioters claimed they would destroy every home in Five Points without a candle burning in the window. Within a short time, every free black home had a burning stick of wax that could be seen from the street.

One Englishman had his eyes gouged after the mob ripped off his ears. Dozens of black and abolitionist churches were destroyed and leveled to the ground. Arthur Tappan's store was the site of several standoffs. The rioting continued for days until the mayor called for the police, all citizens and the military to band together to stop the mob. When the terror ended, vast portions and pillars of the free black community had been destroyed. New York had become a racial war zone.

How well Emily survived is not known, but survive she did.

Chapter 7

New York Funds a Revolution

Webb had a reason to write fake news that would create a mob to stop the abolitionist movement. He had put his money on the theory that a Mexican territory called Texas would become the next big slave-driven economy.

England had started its rocky road to abolition in 1810 when the government outlawed slavery. Loopholes, dissension and poor regulation made the execution of that law hard to implement. Two factions in England were fighting for control over the future of Africans worldwide. The abolitionists who were finding a foothold internationally had control of politics and much of the nation's culture. The banks, however, had control of the world's finances and were happy to fund, invest and circumvent slave laws in order to make money.

In America, the scenario was replicating itself in the battles between Webb and the Tappans. Where the Tappans had taken the abolitionist movement to heart, Webb represented the globalist financial interest. He was a member of the New Washington Association, an investment group hoping to build a port in the burgeoning Texas territory.

The New Washington Association was the result of America's love affair with expansion. At the time it was created, another investor group, the American Land Company, was also organized. Under Charles Butler, it captured $1 million from New Yorkers to promote a migration movement to the Wild West and eventually bought inland property along the San Jacinto River in Texas. The New Washington Association, by contrast, was solely designed to promote the development along the Mexican frontier. Its investors hoped to see the Texas territory break from Mexico and become annexed into the United States. New York society and investors saw Texas as the New South and were ready to get rich by making sure their plan succeeded.

The top New York customs collector, Samuel Swartwout, led the New Washington board of managers. The managers were John Haggarty, Thomas E. Davis and Alexander H. Dana. The association members were the publisher Webb, John B. Austin, John S. Bartlett, William Dall and Stephen Sicard. From Mexico, Lorenzo de Zavala and Joseph Avenzana were members. James Treat, who had been the Mexican consul in New York, was the secretary. The investors bought two schooners to move goods, workers and passengers between New York and Texas.

It was the hope of many global leaders that the land being dubbed the New South would become a plantation economy that could provide the international trade route with cash crops such as cotton and sugar. Mexico owned the land known as Texas, but Webb was not concerned. He was part of a northern movement that supported Texas as a free country and was helping settlers there stage a revolution.

A strong contingent of wealthy New York politicians and businessmen was already backing the South. Success of the agriculture economy depended on plentiful slaves, but it also needed infrastructure, long-term mortgages and land credit. Not only was New York investing in the future of the southern economy, but it was also investing in the slave economy. New York establishment extended credit to plantation owners who needed to buy from the human trafficking industry. To continue to make money, these men had to discredit the work of Jocelyn, Tappan and their colleagues. They, like English banks, needed Texas to become a slave republic.

Mexico outlawed slavery and then rescinded the decision but still never had a great love for it in the land it called Tejas. Its politicians had been willing to turn a blind eye to it in order to get the territory developed. Stephen F. Austin, a Mississippian turned Texan, had become the major land developer, or *empresario*, for the Mexican government. He operated a real estate system that sold property to Americans who wanted to build their own farms and plantations. The Texas economy took hold quickly, and within a decade after he acquired land from Mexico, he was selling it to new settlers by leagues, or one-thousand-acre plots. As a result, settlers created a fast-growing economy in the fertile lands along the Brazos River and the southeast coastal plans.

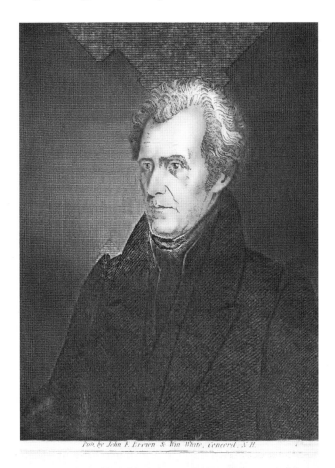

ANDREW JACKSON.

President of the United States.

Portrait of Andrew Jackson. *From* Gen. Andrew Jackson with a Short Sketch of His Life.

Texas captured the fancy and hopes of many ordinary Americans who wanted a chance to build better lives and make money in the foreign country. The sheer number of immigrants flooding into the territory, purchasing land and bringing slaves to work the fields had become a problem for Mexico. Many American immigrants did not meet the criteria the government required. In response, Mexico had begun an organized effort to control, tax and otherwise regulate the new settlers. The Mexican military had a large presence in Texas, and generals would march on towns or engage with settlers in disturbances and skirmishes. As a counter-response, the new residents turned into rebels who began plans to begin a revolution. They would turn Tejas into a sovereign republic called Texas.

A revolution requires guns and ammunition. To obtain these, Austin looked to gain favor from New York political and investment leaders like Webb and his friends. He and other settlers found sympathy with Swartwout. Swartwout was also great friends with the leading Texan rebel, Sam Houston. Houston's friend President Andrew Jackson appointed Swartwout to one of the most coveted posts in New York: customs collector for the Port of New York. Swartwout hosted a series of covert meetings with the Texas revolutionaries. During these clandestine rendezvous, funds were negotiated for arms, equipment and other supplies to support an uprising. Austin was quite vocal in his belief that Texas needed to accomplish two things to corral the land and people into a prosperous economy. First, it needed a strong infrastructure and transportation to control the complex system of waterways that rushed through its fertile lands. Second, the settlers had to be allowed to maintain a slave system to work the plantations. Through Swartwout, Webb and their investment group, he had funding for both.

The Rebel with a Cause

The slavery issue created a consistent undercurrent of tension between Austin and the Mexican government. For some time, those tensions never peaked because development was happening at a quick rate, which made Mexico money and politicians happy. Austin and the settlers, however, had plans to turn Texas into a slave republic as soon as freedom was won.

During the days before the revolution, the New Washington Association planned for a port along the San Jacinto River at the mouth of Galveston Bay to receive the North's supplies of people, guns and ammunition. Austin soon realized he needed a port master. He and the New Washington Association found a kindred spirit in James Morgan, a prosperous merchant who was a rebel with a cause. In Morgan, the New Yorkers had found an ardent supporter of the Texas rebellion and a well-heeled, smart merchant who knew how to move money, goods and people swiftly. He named the schooners the *Flash* and the *Kosciusko* after his son. He also referred to the latter as the *Kos*, his son's nickname. With Morgan at the helm, these schooners and the New Washington Association were set to turn revolution into profit.

Morgan, however, didn't start out to make trouble in Texas; he came to make an honest dollar. When he first saw the growth and economic opportunity that the Mexican-controlled territory was rolling out to Americans, he took an interest in the land. Around 1830, he told his New Orleans business partner to shutter their shop and bring their merchant wares over to Texas. John Reed, his partner, did as he was told. Morgan, meanwhile, bound sixteen slaves as indentured servants to skirt the Mexican slavery ban and headed to the tip of Galveston Bay overland. While Morgan set up shop, Reed headed out on their schooner *Exert*. As Reed came through port, the Mexican customs collector, George Fisher, taxed Reed's haul, and Morgan's tempers flared. He refused to pay because he had been told Mexico would not tax goods entering Texas. From that moment on, Morgan was a Texas rebel and supported the cause of independence.

He set up a profitable shop in Anahuac. His hot defiance of the Mexican government made him a leader in Brazoria and Galveston, two regions that were rising in economic prosperity during the pre–Texas Revolution. His shop had become a popular gathering place for rebels to discuss their plans, vent frustrations and build camaraderie.

As time went on, Morgan became popular and respected. He served in the 1832 Convention, a pivotal moment for the Texas Revolution. He represented Liberty, an eastern rebel community. As the revolution percolated, he set out to create an opportunity for unparalleled wealth. In 1836, he was tapped to become the Texas frontman for the New Washington Association.

Morgan was exactly what New York wanted out of a Texan.

Chapter 8

These Bets Are on Texas

The New Washington Association gave Morgan an enormous amount of power and responsibility. In the October 23, 1835 articles of incorporation, Morgan was named the Texas agent. As such, he was given complete authority to act in the association's name and for its board of managers. An entire article was dedicated to the powers the shareholder held:

That James Morgan, one of the subscribers hereto, possessing the confidence of all the parties hereto, continue to act as the general agent of the company in Texas and is hereby authorized to carry into affect all the projects already contemplated and such further operations as the interest of the company shall be deemed to require from time to time according to his own judgment, exercising such powers and discretion as he may be charged with by the board of managers but subject to their direction in all present and future operations and subject to the general authority of the association to modify, restrict or supersede his powers as agent, to appoint a co-agent or agents or to substitute another in his place.

The final article also limited who could fire him and the constraints on the act:

It is further agreed that the authority to supersede the present General Agent and substitute another in his place as specified in Article 8 belongs solely to the shareholders and not the board of managers and shall not be exercised without just cause as an inefficient or improper management and a decision of two-thirds of the shareholders to that effect after direct notice to said Morgan of the causes alleged and after receiving and considering his answers and explanations in regards thereto on sufficient time given to him to make sense such answers and explanations.

His formal appointment followed his already active involvement with the association. In 1834, he purchased 100,000 acres of southeast coast prairies along Trinity, San Jacinto, Sabine and Nueces Rivers. He also bought property on Galveston Bay to build the port and landing. He hired George Patrick as the storehouse supervisor. Patrick was also the general contractor for repairs at Morgan's house. Patrick was considered one of the most skilled surveyors in Texas, so he was instrumental in helping Morgan find good property to buy. The surveyor could locate and assess lands very well too.

According to Patrick, New Washington was overflowing with cash and incredibly impressive. By the time Morgan returned from New York in December 1835, the development had a packed warehouse and the best inventory along the southeast coast. The association was making profits ranging from 100 percent to 300 percent regularly. Brandy cost Morgan $0.75 per gallon, and he sold it for $3.75. Salt sacks cost him $1.75, and he sold them for $5.00 each. Whether or not Texans knew Morgan was gouging them during the pre-revolution didn't matter. New Washington Association was making money because it had the best inventory within eighty miles.

According to one journalist at the time, New Washington Association was located on the left bank of the San Jacinto on Galveston Bay. Morgan's home was impressive and breathtaking. "In due time the store was built, and the residence, which, without ostentation, might be called a 'mansion,' in a few months afterwards took possession of the summit of the hill. From the east door, a person could see the bay and Morgan's wearing hip, the slanting clipper, the dancing cockboat."

For many decades, Morgan's home was a symbol of Texas success. In 1848, a dozen years after the revolution, a journalist reported that it was still magnificent:

There still the mansion stands with its spotless sides and palings, surrounded with numerous outhouses and negro cottages that mark the nucleus of an extended glebe. The grounds evince the highest state of cultivation, while the rare and precise order of its garden betray the refined care, which at some early period it must have received from a tasteful female hand.

According to the incorporation articles, Morgan was going to hire "laborers from Bermuda" to work on the property and build the projects the board had in mind.

Bermuda in 1835 had recently emancipated its slaves. The United Kingdom had outlawed slavery in 1801, but its colonies were slow to follow the law. But in August 1834, the Bermuda government finally agreed to free its slaves. Once done, the population of Bermuda had 8,818 residents and a slight majority of freed blacks. It had 4,259 white residents and 4,559 freed blacks. Slave owners were compensated for freeing their slaves, but many plantation owners complained that they only received pennies on the dollar.

The former slaves and free blacks were given most rights and privileges of the whites and other citizens, although laws were changed to make it hard for them to vote. The county also had a large population of former slaves who worked at the docks. They were free to be rehired with wages or move on. It was this segment that Morgan wanted to entice as indentured servants to work at the New Washington Association.

The idea that free blacks would want to come to Texas was not farfetched if one believed Mexico would continue to control Texas after the revolution, and many did. In fact, it was common knowledge that Mexican citizens preferred for Texas to remain part of their country. This was the sentiment even as America made many failed attempts to buy it. America sent a round of diplomats to Mexico over the decades. Each offered increasingly higher amounts of money to purchase Texas. Each time, Mexico sent them away with its people's blessings.

According to Benjamin Lundy, a northern abolitionist who was great friends with Jocelyn, the government knew a revolution was afoot, but Mexico intended to defend its territory and win. He wrote, "So much are the Mexicans opposed to it, that a rumor lately obtained credit among them of an attempt by our government to take forcible possession of the territory in question; and Gen. Teran, Minister of War, has been despatched [*sic*] to the north, to enquire into the state of things."

Lundy was a universal emancipationist who aligned himself with the British anti-abolitionist movement. He supported the Londoners and agreed with them that a slave republic would jeopardize their relationship with the United States. These Europeans thought that the United States' attempts to buy Texas were blatant overreach. Lundy quoted the *London Times* in one of his reports:

Portrait of Benjamin Lundy. *From* Life and Travels of Benjamin Lundy.

Without going deep into a delicate subject, we will say that the United States have got far enough to the southward and westward on the Gulf of Mexico, and that it is for the interest and safety of our colonies to have Mexico rather than the United States for their neighbour. The province of Texas ought to remain Mexican, as it is, and not be swallowed up, like the Floridas and the whole course of the Mississippi, by any grasping Government.

Lundy was betting that the United States would never be able to purchase Texas and, if a revolution occurred, the rebels would never win. He expected Mexico would keep control of Texas in some form. He had little respect for

Senator Thomas H. Benton of Missouri, who was an ardent supporter of slavery. Benton had become the spokesperson for the Democratic Party and appealed to a mix of farmers, businessmen and slaveholders. He pushed for the annexation of Texas as a slave state that would expand the plantation system. Lundy evoked his name and alluded to the growing congressional divide on the subject to make his point that Mexico would prevail:

> *It would seem, from the different views here taken of the subject, that the grand project of "Americanus," alias "La Salle," alias Thomas H. Benton, Senator of the United States, and Champion of the Slavite [sic] Faction in this Republic, is not yet likely to be carried into effect.*

And while Mexico had revoked its original edict to outlaw slavery, this did not concern Lundy. Texas, in his mind, could still become a new land for free blacks.

> *We learn that the present government of Mexico has revoked the edict of the late President [Vicente] Guerrero, totally abolishing Slavery, so far as relates to the Province of Texas. The law is, however, still in force prohibiting the further introduction of slaves, and occurring the freedom of all born after a certain period. There are said to be upwards of a thousand slaves in that part of the Mexican Republic, principally taken from the United States. Another very important measure has also been adopted. The Texas country is to be governed, hereafter, as a colony; and the migration of persons from the United States is strictly forbidden, except such as may be specially permitted by the Governor. So much for our meddling with our neighbour's concerns—So much for Benton's disinterested zeal and overflowing patriotism!*

It was this bet that put Lundy on a course to create a distinct free black community in Texas. Mexico still respected the position of the free blacks. They were given equal status as white colonists. As a result, Texas had an appeal for the free black, and like other settlers, they emigrated with the hope for a better life. Lundy was captivated by the idea that free blacks could come to Texas and escape the squalor, riots and general unrest they experienced in the North.

Morgan was aligned with the North's slave supporters, but he knew how to hedge bets. He once thought about becoming a slave smuggler in the years preceding the revolution but decided it was a shortsighted business move. The decision to use paid labor to build New Washington was playing both sides of the fence. At the time, there was no indication that Texas would deny free blacks the same status as white people. The only hint of this was in closed-door sentiments of the revolutionary leadership.

If Texas won the revolution and became a slave state, Morgan had options. He could still purchase slaves and turn his free black labor into slaves. Or, if the state allowed free blacks, they could continue to have their rights and he'd pay them. If Texas lost, he would be able to continue to build New Washington using contract labor and indentured servants. Morgan was not above using any and all methods to hire blacks to make money or purchase them for the same reason.

Lundy had bets on Mexico, and Morgan was hedging his bets on Texas.

Chapter 9

The Free Black Colony of Texas

Between 1830 and 1835, Lundy visited Texas three times. He had high hopes of creating his free black colony west of the Colorado River. In 1833, he made his second trip after he visited a free black colony in Canada where he was inspired. His Texas trek began in May when he landed on the banks of the Brazos River. He wrote, "The water of the river here is of a real vermilion colour. For the first few miles from the sea, the river is bordered with marshes or plains, destitute of wood; above these, timber of various kinds abounds, among which the live oak is very common. I saw, this morning, a young alligator walking along the shore."

Lundy enjoyed Texas. He soaked up the atmosphere and grew to enjoy its people and culture. He fought cholera and other disease on his travels. He battled ants and encountered the dreaded Texas mosquitoes. Even after he had been robbed many times, he didn't judge Texans. Even when mobs attempted to attack him, he believed they just disagreed with him about his views on Mexican rule. When he needed money, he reverted to his former trade, saddle repair. He visited with many prominent Texas residents, such as Samuel Williams. He said they were mostly kind to him. He also met with free blacks who described their life in the Mexican territory and noticed that racial equality in pre-revolutionary Texas was well established. He described his conversations with them:

There lives here, in Bexar, a free black man, who speaks English. He came as a slave, first from North Carolina to Georgia, and then from Georgia to

Nacogdoches, in Texas. There his master died, and the heirs sold him to another person. This new master, being apprehended for debt, offered the slave his freedom if he would take him out of prison. The slave complied, but the mas'er dying soon after, an attempt was made by his heirs to re-enslave the man, which however proved unsuccessful. He now works as a blacksmith in this place. He is highly pleased with my plans. Though he is jet-black, he says the Mexicans pay him the same respect as to other laboring people, there being no difference made here on account of colour.

He was also impressed with the amount of education and wealth free blacks had in Texas.

I walked out this forenoon with Matthew Thomas, to see the cane patch, grounds, (and etc…) of his father-in-law, Felipe Elua, a black Louisiana creole, who was formerly a slave, but who has purchased the freedom of himself and family. He has resided here twenty-six years, and he now owns five or six houses and lots, besides a fine piece of land near town. He has educated his children so that they can read and write, and speak Spanish as well as French. They are all fine looking, smart black people. He has a sister also residing in Bexar, who is married to a Frenchman. The sugar cane, of which there is a patch of about an acre on Elua's land, looks as well as that which grows in Hayti, and the land is evidently well adapted to it. The frost does not kill the roots of the plant here as it does further north, but the sprouts make their appearance in the spring, so that it is unnecessary to replant. Besides the cane, we saw some fine looking cotton, a large patch of sweet potatoes, together with beans and other garden vegetables, the property of the same black man, and all in beautiful order.

By November, Lundy had secured a meeting with the governor, who was agreeable to his plan. Lundy found him more liberal than he expected and was even pleased when the governor wanted to read his newspaper and writings. Lundy reported:

This morning I had my official interview with the governor, presented my credentials, and explained to him the general scope of my views. I found him frank and communicative, and still more friendly than at our former interview. He approves highly of my proposals, and assures me that he will grant me any land within his prerogative, as soon as the law of 1830 shall have been repealed. He promises to give me information of the repeal immediately on receiving it, and assures me that no other application which maybe made to him shall take precedence of mine. He says that if the general Congress, now in session, should fail to repeal the law in question, the State Legislature will make a strong appeal to it in favour of the measure; and he feels sure that the professors of the various sects in religion will henceforth be admitted as settlers, without any restriction in regard to their faith.

Several meetings, a few missed visits due to illness, a few months of unpredictable Texas weather and several sleepless nights later, Lundy received his colonization grant on February 3, 1834. The contract was similar to others issued that year. He had 138,000 acres and could bring 250 families. He described the terms when he wrote:

Comformably [sic] *to the governor's interpretation, the Council of State consented to let me have a grant of thirty leagues and thirty labons of land, on condition that I settle, on the same land, two hundred and fifty families: the land to be mine, and I to make such terms as I please with the settlers, either as purchasers, doners, or tenants. But the government will not give to these settlers any other lands, although, to those who come at their own expense, and ask for land, it will give what the law specifies.*

Throughout his trip, Mexican government officials expressed support for a free black colony in Texas. By December, Lundy had even found free blacks in Texas who would be willing to move into his proposed colony. He wrote, "In the afternoon I called by invitation at the house of Henry Powell, a very intelligent and respectable coloured man, who migrated hither from Louisiana. He takes a deep interest in my enterprise, and will join as a settler, immediately, when I commence a colony."

By March 21, 1835, Lundy had received the translated final contract. The governor also answered the last of his questions. The results surprised him: "From these answers it appears that I cannot locate my grant of land until I bring on a part of the settlers! This information, which I had not anticipated, will render it necessary for me to hurry home and expedite the migration as fast as possible."

With that, Lundy headed back to the United States. Texas was about to have a free black colony, and he needed to find people to live in it.

Chapter 10

Emily in Texas

etween June and December 1835, Lundy's vision for a free black colony in Texas was well received. Even on his trip back to New York, he learned that he might be able to help former slaves who had been freed. All he had to do was convince courts that the idea had merit so they could migrate as free blacks. Within one month after he left Texas, he had found support. On June 13, 1835, he stopped along the Mississippi River in Nashville to visit a widow he knew and some friends.

Some coloured people in this vicinity, were lately emancipated by the will of Donnelson, the elder brother of Gen. Jackson's wife; but the court decided that their emancipation was illegal, and that they must be held as slaves by the heirs, unless they would leave the United States. The acting executor says he is about to send them to Africa. The coloured people, however, fear to go there, and are apprehensive that the executor will still keep them in bondage, if he can; they have therefore applied to me, through the agency of a friend, for an opportunity to go to my colony. I have visited Stokely Donnelson, who has them in charge and conversed with him on the subject. He says that he has no objection to their going to my colony, if the Court will agree to it. My friend Bryant has undertaken to attend to the business in my absence.

For Emily, however, the summer of 1835 was not any less riotous than the year before. The Tappans led the abolitionists on a massive publicity campaign. They spread about one million pieces of antislavery materials throughout the nation. By the time Lundy had completed his voyage to the United States, proslave riots raged in Boston, Philadelphia and New York. About 150 anti-abolitionist riots occurred in 1835. In August, the bloodiest incident since the Nat Turner Rebellion erupted when whites became angry that free blacks were creating competition for jobs.

For three days, Washington, D.C., erupted in riot. Whites first destroyed Beverly Snow's Epicurean Eating House, which a free black man owned. It was a sophisticated and well-respected restaurant. Snow was educated, married, wealthy and successful, much like King Lanson had been. Whites destroyed any business that a free black owned, including schools and churches. The riots ended on August 9 when President Andrew Jackson brought in the military to quash the violence.

The state of the abolitionist movement weighed on many people. Davy Crockett, who was a congressman representing Tennessee, was anti-Jackson and populist in his views. He was also an ardent opponent of Martin Van Buren and the Indian Removal Act. He had a snarky style and quick wit. By 1835, his snark was on display during a belittling report on Five Points, where Van Buren had a huge following.

Crockett had enemies in Congress who eventually caused him to abandon politics. He never said whether he was an abolitionist or a proslavery advocate, although he represented a slave state. He did, however, blame political gamesmanship for the country's inability to come to agreement on the issue. He said, "I offer gentlemen, the abolition of slavery: Let the work begin in the two houses of Congress. There are no slaves in the country more servile than the party slaves in Congress." Once it was clear that his political career was over, he made plans to head to Texas.

So did Emily. Jocelyn sometimes wrote for Lundy's publication, the *Liberator*. That meant he and Emily both knew about the plans to create a free black colony in Texas. Abolitionists argued over the visions for free black colonies, but in this case, even anti-abolitionists like Webb were exploring the idea that Texas could be a place for free blacks to live. The New Washington Association had a vision for a free black colony filled with newly freed slaves from Bermuda. Morgan, however, was having a hard time working with Bermuda officials who did not trust the Texas rebels' commitment to an antislavery economy, and eventually, he stopped working with them.

It remains unclear how Emily and Morgan ever met or what they spoke about. It also remains unclear what conversations Jocelyn had with Morgan or what was stated in their conversations. Nonetheless, Emily decided to

Portrait of Davy Crockett. *Courtesy of S.S. Osgood.*

work for Morgan at New Washington. In October, Emily and Jocelyn met Morgan in a porter-side coffeehouse, where she signed an employment contract to work in Texas. Morgan's attorney, Frederick Platt, drew a one-year contract for Emily. She would earn $100 annually.

> *This agreement, made & entered into by and between Emily West of New Haven, Conn. of the one part & James Morgan of Texas of the other part, Witnesseth that the said West, hereby binds herself that she will go out in said Morgan's Vessel to Texas and there work for said Morgan at any kind of house work she, said West is qualified to do and to industriously pursue the same from the time she commences until the end of twelve months and not to quit or leave said Morgan's employ after she commences work for him, at any time whatever, without said Morgan's consent, until the end of twelve months aforesaid, said Morgan hereby binding himself to the said West out to Texas, on board said Morgan's vessel, free of expense, and to set said West to work within one week after she gets there if not sooner, said Morgan agreeing to pay said West at the rate of one hundred dollars pr. year, said Wages to be paid every three months if required.*
>
> *In witness thereof the parties have hereunto set their hands and seal in New York this 5th day of October 1835. In the presence of Frederick Platt, Simeon L. Jacilyn, J Morgan, Emily D West.*

Emily had to have been influenced by Lundy's promise of his free black colony. He was actively promoting the idea and seeking his 250 new residents when she signed her contract. The idea of a free and peaceful life in Texas had to have been attractive. Texas would be relief from Five Points and the institutionalized discrimination she faced in New York. When she left, Lundy had not started the colony and wasn't sure when he would. Northern riots illuminated the anger that whites had toward free blacks. The damage done in Five Points displaced many people, so Lundy's plan had to have been popular.

Meanwhile, Jocelyn and Webb, Morgan's associate investor, remained enemies. But that didn't change the fact that the Mexican territory enticed free blacks who did not want to be pushed into an African colony. Emily wasn't the only one to sign a contract with Morgan. Three free blacks and some Scottish Highlanders signed contracts. Her friend Diana Leonard, a washerwoman, also signed a contract. They boarded the *Flash*, the New Washington vessel that Morgan used, and headed to Texas.

By Christmas, they were working on a profitable venture. According to Patrick, his overseer, Morgan sold $12,370.02 worth of goods between the dawn of the Texas Revolution and the Siege of 1836. The port was a booming business that was moving New York goods to Texas settlers. Emily and the others probably didn't feel the effects of the budding war for some time even though Morgan had become a central figure in the rebel cause. Because the Mexican forces showed restraint early on against Texas, Emily and her coworkers probably thought they could work peacefully throughout these precursor entanglements and settle their differences. In fact, the New York investors also hoped for a peaceful resolution even as they discussed funding a revolution, albeit they wanted a different result.

It would have been easy for Emily and her coworkers to know the temperament of the Texans. Morgan's merchant shop and New Washington were popular rebel gathering spots. Because of his popularity as a rebel, Morgan was involved in almost all the pre-revolution scrimmages and standoffs. He was involved in the disturbance at Fort Anahuac, an early standoff that happened after his friend William B. Travis tricked the Mexican forces. In that case, the Mexican forces allowed rebel militia to bring through a cannon, knowing it could be used against other Mexican forces when the troops reached Anahuac. Eventually, though, the Mexican government would become more irritated. Within a few months, Santa Anna would begin his advance. After that, there could not have been any misunderstandings.

Emily had moved from her home full of war zones to a territory full of war.

Chapter 11

Dysfunctional Texans

Lundy's hope for a free black colony rested in the idea that Texas would remain a Mexican territory. He had already been warned that Stephen F. Austin might not be trusted to help him if the rebels won. The day before Lundy met with the Mexican governor, he heard that Austin was not an abolitionist or an idealist. Lundy needed to be wary of anything Austin said. "One of my acquaintances here informs me, that, in his opinion, Stephen F. Austin acts a double part in every thing. He says that Austin once told him that it was necessary to practise duplicity in dealing with the Mexicans."

As a result, Lundy spent a good deal of time watching the revolution unfold and following the actions. He developed critical opinions about the rebels and always remained supportive of Mexico.

Pre-revolutionary Texas had two groups of settlers. One was the war party. Its leaders were the Williamsons, the Whartons, Henry Smith, Branch T. Archer, William B. Travis, Jim Bowie, Edward Burleson, J.D. Patrick, Asa Hoxey and Alexander Horton. Morgan was also among these men. They were labeled liberals and were actively organizing a militia for revolution. The other group was conservative. These men were labeled the peace party. It was this group that Lundy supported. The peace party preferred deliberation, negotiation and constitutional remedies to work out a deal with Mexico. Over time, however, these thinkers realized a war would come. Therefore, they dedicated themselves to limiting the damage a revolution would cause Texas. Only a scant few settlers preferred to leave Mexico with an absolute authority over them. During Lundy's last trip to Texas, he met with Samuel Williams, who was a peace party member. Williams, he said, spoke with reason. "He is no mad revolutionist. In his opinion, Texas will not very soon become a separate State."

Given Williams's sentiment, Lundy likely convinced Jocelyn and others that Texas would have a war, but it might not have independence. That meant that if all went well, Emily would be in Texas, where she could be among the first settlers in Lundy's new free black colony. If so, the hope would have been to live in peace and equality with white people.

From the moment they arrived at New Washington, Emily and her friends were watching the Mexican forces change their attitude toward the settlers. Government restraint was being replaced with military advances. The campaign of 1835 was in its last weeks upon their arrival, and even though Texas had the upper hand, Mexico was still the larger and more organized force. In December 1835, General Sam Houston had been given the authority to organize an army. At first, regular army soldiers and volunteers would each receive 640 acres for serving, but later, the provisional government increased the land to 800 acres for the soldiers. Public meetings were held throughout December. The fervor at these meetings intensified as more settlers joined the war party's philosophy. A territory-wide consensus was growing that absolute independence was the only answer against Mexico's rule.

Victory, however, was not a given. Sometimes, even with the upper hand, the Texas troops and their provisional government made bad decisions. Back in the North, any abolitionist would have believed Mexico could prevail against the coastal gaggle of dysfunctional Americans. In January 1836, James Fannin and Francis Johnson began a long campaign with a band of soldiers and volunteers. They planned to stage an attack at the strategic and prosperous port of Matamoras along the lower Rio Grande. Capturing the town would help offset the cost of the war and bolster the floundering provisional government. The Texas settlers were poor, and the government had no way to raise funds for a revolution. Finances were always a struggle.

Private speculative funds from investors were imperative for the war effort and the subsequent recovery. These funds were so critical that leaders had to craft messages so the settlers wouldn't see the revolution as an "investors' war." Public loans from the United States were also always being sought. Raised funds were used to pay for supplies, food, guns, cannons and ammunition the troops would need. This meant the New Washington Association, with its New York backers, was an incredibly important development for the

After a daguerreotype by B. P. Paige.

SAM HOUSTON

Portrait of Sam Houston. *Author's collection, from the public domain.*

settlers and their army. At New Washington, Emily had firsthand knowledge of the troops' movements and how the war was progressing.

When she arrived, Mexico was taking back towns, like Bexar, that Texas had captured earlier. With six thousand troops, Santa Anna and his cadre of commanders began to easily quash rebel forces. Also, the Matamoras Expedition, which was a Texas attempt to take the town of Matamoras, was a bristling bust, and many men died under the power of the Mexican troops. A convoluted bungle of political games, military decisions and colossal egos collided during the expedition to deliver a major Texas defeat. The bungle gave Santa Anna a boost that unified his troops. Decades later in 1899, the decision to march on Matamoras was considered a horrible move. Historian Dudley Wooten reviewed the lingering effects of Matamoros and how the disaster emboldened Santa Anna:

All the confusion and disaster that followed in the spring of 1836 were traceable to this Matamoros scheme and the arbitrary action of the council in regard to it. The troops were stationed throughout the western country under separate chiefs, the soldiers were in doubt as to what would be the next move, the officers were involved in controversies with the government and with each other, and what should have been a united and well organized army under one competent commander became a disorganized and discordant force, made up of widely scattered detachments engaged in pushing the individual plans of their several leaders. The fall of the Alamo and the massacre at Goliad were among the terrible results of such a policy.

The government and military dysfunction wore on the settlers. The public at large became disenchanted even as Austin gave rousing speeches along the Mississippi River. According to Wooten, the settlers' sunken spirit was hard to overcome. The real threat of a massive army advancing on them couldn't even ignite any energy. "The people at large, however, seemed strangely indifferent to the approaching danger, and it was with the greatest difficulty they could be aroused. This was largely due to the general disgust at the provisional government and its unseemly discords, which continued to paralyze the army and dishearten everybody."

Despite the irritation with their leaders, the settlers still voted in February 1835 to send delegates to Washington-on-the-Brazos. The delegates would meet in March and begin the documents for a new and independent government free from Mexico. Emily's boss, Morgan, was about to become a commanding officer in a revolutionary war.

If Emily was writing to Jocelyn during this time, she certainly had a lot to tell him. Jocelyn, in turn, would have had a lot to tell Lundy, who was probably happy to hear it.

Chapter 12

The Runaway Scrape

W hen Santa Anna began his advance in 1836, Lundy was hopeful but uncertain that Texas would remain under Mexican control. He did not, however, trust Austin and his gamesmanship, so he was nervous. What Emily would have thought under the circumstances is unknown, but she was clearly in a precarious position. She was working for a man with known anti-abolitionist ties, and she was still in the early months of her contract. Only one thing was certain. Within sixteen weeks of their arrival, Emily and her coworkers were working at a port that was supplying a revolution. An estimated five thousand people lived in the town surrounding the port landing.

Meanwhile, at Washington-on-the-Brazos, the delegates elected Houston as the supreme commander of the military forces. Under his command, current troops would receive 1,280 acres if they remained through the war. Those who served six months would receive 640 acres. Three months of service rendered 340 acres. New recruits who served between six months and on to the end of the war would receive 940 acres. Among one of Houston's first acts was to send out a call to the United States for troops, money and supplies. The country responded, and volunteers from throughout the South arrived to fight for Texas. Many of them arrived in New Washington.

Once he was elected, Houston immediately set out for Gonzalez, where most of his troops were stationed. Houston soon realized they were all a bunch of ragamuffins. They weren't trained and had few weapons but were full of bravado. More men were arriving daily from other communities and

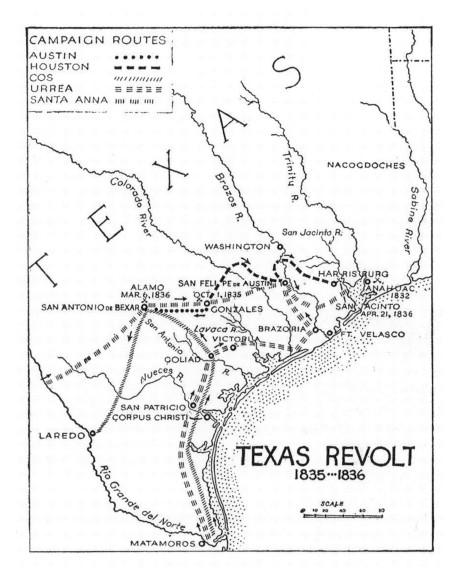

Drawn in 1927, this map shows the Mexican and rebel campaign routes during the Texas Revolution. *From* Pageant of America, *vol. 2,* The Lure of the Frontier *(1928).*

the United States. By the time he reached Gonzalez, the troops had already had one standoff with the Mexican military. When it was finished, they had a cannon, originally on loan to the Texans to fight the Indians. Mexico wanted it back, but the small militia didn't give it to them. Rather than fight the Texans over a small cannon, Mexico retreated. Texas was delighted. In celebration, the cannon was outfitted with wheels and filled with gunpowder, and a flag was put atop it. The ragtag flag read, "Come and Take It." It stood as a moniker for the settlers' grit.

When Houston arrived on March 11, he was unaware that the Alamo had fallen on March 6. He was preparing to march the Gonzalez troops to Bexar to help Travis and the men at the mission. When he heard about the massacre, he was grief-stricken. News traveled slowly, and the troops often fought in isolation with no knowledge of what the others were facing. Most settlers who lived east of the Colorado and between the Brazos and Galveston Bay heard about the bloody defeats at the Alamo and Goliad many days after they happened. Couriers were sent to tell them how battles were fought and their outcomes. Many times in 1836, they would hear that Houston would retreat rather than fight, and if Texas lost a battle, Santa Anna left no prisoners.

When Gonzalez settlers heard the Alamo had fallen, they went into a panic. Historian Dudley Wooten recalled decades later, "Women and children, many of them widows and orphans by the butchery at San Antonio, were wild with fear of the approaching Mexicans. It was then that the universal panic began which, spreading afterwards as Houston retired to the east, was known among the old settlers as the 'Runaway Scrape.'"

Houston learned that Santa Anna was heading to Gonzalez, so the Texan began a strategic retreat. This would become a trademark move he would use throughout the siege that gave him time to train the men who were now his troops. Meanwhile, the townspeople began to hear about the Mexican advance and the constant Texas retreat. They began a mass evacuation toward the east. Some men went to war, and the rest gathered their families and fled.

First the evacuees learned about the deaths that led to the Alamo and the details of that mission. While they were still grieving and trying to process the Alamo, they learned about a particularly horrid massacre at Goliad, where James Fannin was in command. Fannin surrendered on Palm Sunday, twenty days after the Alamo fell. He and his men assumed they would become prisoners, but they didn't. Mexico instead lined between 425 and 445 Texans between two rows of soldiers and massacred them. The prisoners were shot at point-blank range. Those who survived were clubbed and knifed to death. Then, the Mexicans went inside the Goliad fort and killed the men who were lame from battle. Fannin, who watched hundreds upon hundreds of his troops die, was then led into the courtyard, where he was blindfolded and tied to a chair. His last thoughts were of his family and his faith. He wanted his family to have his belongings, and he wanted a Christian burial. Neither was granted. His body was burned with the bodies of the other Texans killed that day.

This culmination of unexpectedly gruesome stories fueled the evacuation called the Runaway Scrape. It began as a small refugee movement until January 1836, when Santa Anna's troops marched on San Antonio de Bexar. It grew wild and unorganized as reports became exaggerations filled with fake news. The reports fed the fear that Santa Anna would kill civilians. The evacuation was compounded by the soggy coastal Texas climate, where streams were raging, mud was deep and movement was slow and dangerous. Santa Anna never gave any indication that he intended to harm settlers, but the perception that he could was very real in the collective minds of Texans. Wooten recalled the effects of the stories: "By the time the Runaway Scrape reached Galveston Bay, the entire territory was in a panic. Texas settlers were horrified at the news of the defeated campaign. They were in terror when they heard the details about the deaths of hundreds of volunteers and soldiers."

During the Runaway Scrape, New Washington Association was pivotal in the refugee evacuation. Morgan and his crew actively moved settlers to Galveston and out of the territory, using the *Flash*. It was an impressive schooner that moved fast in the waters, but it was also smaller than most vessels of the day. They also used the *Kos*. These schooners, along with the *Cayuga* and every other Texas vessel, swept the rivers in anticipation of the Mexican army's arrival. During the evacuation, Texans in Nacogdoches intercepted orders that the Mexican army would shoot anyone who had a gun and force everyone else to flee.

On March 20, Morgan was named the commander of Galveston Island, where many of the settlers were being sent to evacuate. When he was called to duty, he left Emily and her coworkers at New Washington. Like most who did not go to war, they were expected to fend for themselves as best they could. They could evacuate. They could stay and face the Mexicans. In Emily's case, she appears to have stayed to operate the major port. It appears the residents of New Washington also stayed in town when the military campaigns were in their early stages. At the height of the revolution, the *Flash* arrived with hauls of war volunteers from around the United States. It was also used to bring supplies and other necessities for the revolution. The cannon called the Twin Sisters arrived on the *Flash*.

Some accounts claim Emily was a manager at the port during this time. Others state she was probably a simple washerwoman like her friend Diane.

Others speculate that she may have managed the hotel or one of the buildings. She may have been a manager, a laborer, a clerk and so much more. Emily was working at a major war port during the height of a revolution. Her boss was gone. No one knew when or if he would return. She may very well have done what every other Texas woman did in those days.

She did whatever it took to get the job done.

Chapter 13

The Burning of New Washington

Emily was at New Washington when Santa Anna's first troops arrived looking for Judge David Burnet.

Judge Burnet lived quietly a few miles from Lynchburg, where he had a home on Burnet Bay. The bay was just miles inland from the New Washington port. He eventually sold some of his property to the New York investor group the American Land Company. It was a competitor of the New Washington Association.

Burnet was not originally politically active but rose to unlikely prominence when he heard that Santa Anna had been appointed the Mexican dictator. Because no one else wanted to be president of the Republic of Texas, in 1836, he was elected. Delegates elected him at the Convention of 1836 with seven rising votes. He was a reluctant president between March 17 and October 22 that year. He often angered Sam Houston, the political delegates and the public at large. Despite Burnet's unpopularity, Santa Anna made finding him and his government one of Mexico's great missions.

Burnet gave Texans great anxiety over the location of the government headquarters because he kept moving it throughout the siege. Originally stationed at Washington-on-the-Brazos, he moved it for a few moments to New Washington. Then Burnet and Houston became at odds after the Goliad Massacre, and Burnet moved it again. Houston's strategic retreats to train troops exasperated Burnet, like most Texans at the time. The president simply couldn't figure out what Houston was thinking. During this state of utter perplexity, Burnet moved the headquarters to Harrisburg. Then, he quickly decided the government should become part of the Runaway Scrape. So, the leaders packed up and returned to New Washington. From there, they would sail to Galveston Island on one of the port's schooners.

The fact that two prominent leaders of the revolution were not working together was clear to the settlers and had a deep effect on the community. Their disconnected relationship exacerbated the Runaway Scrape, which was already stressing settlers who were fighting the soggy Texas coastal climate, according to Wooten.

> The weather was wretched; the rain poured in torrents, the roads were quagmires, the prairies were trackless seas of water, the streams were swollen and swift, and the dull and lowering skies covered everything like a pall of gloom and despair. The "Runaway Scrape" had begun in earnest, and the frightened colonists, seeing in Houston's retreat and the removal of the government to Harrisburg sure Mexican conquest of the whole country, fled in wild confusion, spreading dismay and dread everywhere they came.

Never mind that the revolutionary deserters ran amok among the towns as they tried to justify their decisions, Wooten continued.

> The wretchedness and desperation of those times were frightful, and the women and children suffered most. The greatest terror was caused by some cowardly deserters, who left the army and ran through the country, even to Eastern Texas, circulating the most outrageous accounts of the size of Santa Anna's forces and the retreat of the Texan troops.

While deserters embellished Santa Anna's army and added fuel to Houston's controversial military strategy, Burnet caused the dictator to change his battle plans. Originally, Santa Anna planned to meet Houston at Groce's plantation, where the troops were preparing the Twin Sisters, the cannon that was a gift from the people of Cincinnati. When Santa Anna heard that Burnet also traveled with Lorenzo de Zavala, a mortal enemy of Santa Anna, the general decided to start chasing the rebel president. De Zavala, a Mexican citizen who also invested in New Washington Association, knew the general well enough to predict his moves. Santa Anna headed to Harrisburg to look for them.

On April 15, Santa Anna and fifteen dragoons walked into Harrisburg, where they captured two townspeople who told them the leaders had already left. Harrisburg was a timber port that exported to the United States and

Mexico. It also delivered supplies to San Felipe through Harrisburg by water and then overland to the Brazos River. The next day, the Mexican troops stayed in town. They ransacked homes and burned them to the ground, according to Colonel Pedro Delgado, who was one of Santa Anna's staff members. Townspeople who were hiding in the woods saw the event and began firing on the Mexicans.

> *After the houses had been sacked and burnt down, a party of Americans fired upon our men from the woods; it is wonderful that some of us, camped as we were along the bank of the bayou, were not killed. The Quartermaster-Sergeant of Matamoros was seriously wounded. This incident took place at 5 o'clock P.M. On the same day Colonel Almonte started from Harrisburg for New Washington with the cavalry.*

Upon the reports that the president and interim government were heading to New Washington, Santa Anna sent Adjunct General Juan Almonte and a squadron to find and capture them. Almonte was almost successful. Burnet and the others had gotten on a schooner as the Mexican troops approached. They were still within shooting distance when Almonte saw them from the shore. One troop drew his gun and aimed. Almonte and the rest of the troops saw women on board. Burnet's wife was holding a baby alongside the other women. Almonte told the soldier to stand down, and the passengers sailed on to Galveston Island in peace. Upon arrival, they met Morgan, who was now a colonel in charge of the city. They likely told Morgan about Santa Anna's attempts to capture them and his march to New Washington after he burned Harrisburg to the ground.

On April 18, while Morgan continued to send schooners to New Washington, Sam Houston arrived at Harrisburg and saw the devastation himself. Def Smith, one of Houston's spies, captured a courier who told them where Santa Anna was. The general and his men were below Harrisburg, right in front of them. The courier also had papers that contained Santa Anna's military plans. Once Houston got the papers and studied them, he ordered his troops toward Lynch's Ferry for a showdown. Santa Anna's position was within the narrow peninsula of the river, which left him pinned and trapped. Houston left the wagons they didn't need. He left the baggage and anything not needed for battle. He ordered seventy-five men to guard the sick, rallied the rest of the troops and went after Santa Anna. The men marched fast and hard with the cannon. A settler gave them floorboards and lumber to repair an old ferryboat so they could move the Twin Sisters cannon over the bayou in their rush to meet the Mexican army. The effort took an entire day. They marched in mud and water. They pushed on without breaks or meals for days until Houston made camp under a grove and let them rest.

Meanwhile, Santa Anna and his army arrived in New Washington at noon the next day. He learned about Almonte's decision to let Burnet and his team escape. Almonte had a history of protecting Texas civilians and women during war. Susanna Dickinson, who survived the Alamo, claimed at one point that Almonte talked Santa Anna out of imprisoning her, although that tale might have been embellished in later years. She also said in her earlier accounts that Santa Anna decided she needed to be released to Houston, so he instructed Almonte, who spoke very good English, to accompany and protect her during the journey. Santa Anna probably understood Almonte's decision not to shoot Burnet, even if he didn't like it.

While at New Washington, the Mexican troops found flour, soap, tobacco and many "articles" that Delgado said were given to Santa Anna. The general sent Delgado to find beeves. He said they were so plentiful around New Washington that he returned with one hundred heads. They slaughtered cattle, seized horses and took boats. On Santa Anna's command, Delgado led the effort to destroy everything that was in the warehouses and burn all the buildings to the ground. During their plunder, they loaded a flatboat with flour and supplies and set it afloat with a sail to retrieve it later.

> On the 20th, at about 8 o'clock A.M. everything was ready for the march. We had burnt a fine warehouse on the wharf, and all the houses in the town, when Captain Barragan rushed in at full speed, reporting that Houston was close on our rear, and that his troops had captured some of our stragglers, and had disarmed and dispatched them.

Emily was at the port when Santa Anna arrived. She was at the takeover and burning. Her other friends, such as Diane the laborer, aren't mentioned, but they may have been there as well. While Santa Anna's troops moved on New Washington, the townspeople fled on the schooners to Galveston, exasperating the mass exodus at the port. The Runaway Scrape also included slaves being housed in a local smuggling warehouse. Most of them were children whom the Texas slave smuggler Monroe Edwards owned. Edwards had been an apprentice of Morgan's years earlier, and the colonel's team oftentimes allowed Edwards to board his hundreds of slaves before the settlers.

Delgado does not mention that townspeople tried to attack the Mexicans like Harrisburg residents had. By the time they arrived, he writes as though only the port workers remained. It was this moment in the war that changed Emily's fate and began her legacy.

Santa Anna took her—and possibly others—as a prisoner of war when he left the charred remains of New Washington behind.

The Beginning of the Showdown

While at New Washington, Santa Anna decided not to chase Burnet to Galveston Island. Instead, Santa Anna decided to turn around and head east despite the capture of his courier. This meant he would meet Houston at Lynch's Ferry, which he'd passed on his way to New Washington. As they neared Anahuac, Santa Anna stumbled upon a Texas reconnaissance force. They began an exchange on the land where Buffalo Bayou and the San Jacinto River meet. Texan Sydney Sherman and his small force skirmished with the Mexicans until the event almost escalated into a battle. Two Texans were wounded; one of them died later. With the heat on, Sherman began a retreat and returned to Houston's camp to report the encounter. Once the situation diffused, Santa Anna made camp. He built several fortifications with baggage, boxes and packs. He left the centers open for the artillery and infantry. His cavalry was on the right, and his last line extended all the way to the timber along the river.

Just days earlier, Emily had watched her new home burn to the ground. Now, she found herself in a fiery skirmish that was a prelude to a war battle. The event had to have had some similarities to the riots she experienced in New York. That didn't mean, however, that she'd seen it all.

A showdown was about to happen, and Emily was situated right in the center of the Mexican artillery.

Chapter 14

Seventy-Two Hours and a Tent

S an Jacinto was a beautiful sight. The waters of the bayou were deep and skirted by live oaks decorated with dangling festoons of soft, gray moss that climbed from the giant trunks and spread across vast limbs. Buffalo Bayou was deep and sluggish and covered with tall, waving grass where small tree groves lined it in no order. Wooten, the late nineteenth-century historian, wrote that in late April, the heroic site celebrated the twilight of the spring season in fantastic display:

> *Beyond this lay the Gulf marshes of the San Jacinto Bay, treacherous and miry, and covered with a thick growth of rank verdure and swampy timber. The wet and late spring was now ripening into early summer, the atmosphere was soft and balmy, the trees and grass were fresh and fragrant, and the whole scene was full of those sights and sounds that make life sweet and hope strong in human breasts.*

Here was picturesque land where the Mexican and Texan troops made their camp and prepared for a battle where neither would retreat. Texas prepared under a grove of live oaks with the river timber and the bayou surrounding them. Mexico prepared on the coastal prairie above them. If the Texans scuttled for a look on the rise that the open prairie was on, they could see the camp, its fortifications and troop movements.

In addition to officers and troops, Mexican military camps featured a cadre of civilians who worked for them as they went to war. The military traveled in the style of European armies. This meant they traveled like an organized society. Officers lived on the battlefield in large and elaborate officer tents. They had rooms and furnishings inside their tents. They also had a staff. The social structure was clear and defined. Members understood the roles they played and the limitations of their stations. The civilians were called camp followers. Many of them were women. Women had a distinctive place as camp followers since the earliest days of the Mexican military. Depending on the role, a woman may or may not have fought in battles. An umbrella term, *soldaderas*, has also been used to describe these women and the part they played in the Mexican army.

The first group were actual members of the troops' families. They were wives, sisters, cousins and so forth. They cared for the troop they were following. The second group were the laborers. These were working women who would perform traditional female jobs. They would wash clothes, make meals, clean and sew. They set up camp and cleaned weapons. In some cases, they were termed "washerwomen," and they were paid to maintain regular household duties for a troop. In other cases, the washerwomen were also paid for sexual favors, like a wife. These two groups were not seen as war participants or considered to have a stake in the outcome of the war.

However, the third group of women was made up of active paramilitary. These women were skilled in military maneuvers. They fought in combat and knew how to shoot weapons. They usually did not have a formal rank, although they might occasionally rise to an informal officer title and even have a few men under their command.

Mexican military life for the average soldier was harsh, and camp followers provided some relief for him. While the army had a priest in its camp, it did not have a doctor. If a soldier was wounded on the battlefield, the government offered no medical assistance. Camp followers were expected to care for him, or he suffered and fended for himself. Washerwomen were necessary because the government made no provision to feed, house or care for the troops. The role that these women played was incredibly important. They were left to handle the logistics required to maintain camp. It was not uncommon for the commanders and troops to not even concern themselves with the details required to construct or take down a camp. The camp followers did it.

Santa Anna was also known to have little sympathy for the common troops and considered them to be simple tools that he needed to execute his war vision. In 1836, Mexican commanders often had food, adequate shelter and payment for their service. The troops, however, were required to find their own food with their camp followers. This meant they would have to hunt and scour the wilderness while the commanders' staff cooked and prepared them meals.

Emily spent roughly seventy-two hours as a prisoner of war. She could not have had enough time to learn about camp life or how to become a camp follower. Besides, she didn't even meet the criteria to belong to any of these groups. Most washerwomen and camp followers were illiterate and uneducated; she was educated and could read and write. They spoke Spanish; she spoke English. The chances that she ever spoke meaningfully to a camp follower had to be remote. Camp followers who served Santa Anna as his staff did routinely enter his tent, like Delgado. A batman, or a valet, would always be on hand. Women servants also entered his tent at the battle camp. An unnamed Texas spy reported that he saw a woman giving Santa Anna champagne and breakfast in his tent. The spy, who may have been Def Smith, did not name the woman, but Houston grumbled that he hoped she would keep the general occupied.

Santa Anna was a European-style soldier, and while he may have been a womanizer, he was also aware of his role as a military leader. He'd been trained to follow the Spanish and French battle tactics. His approach to civilians, prisoners and the enemy was influenced and seen through the lens by which he was trained. He traveled with his regular officers as he searched for Burnet. This meant he surrounded himself with soldiers who were trained like he was.

After the burnings of Harrisburg and New Washington, Santa Anna would have taken any prisoners and held them according to the cultural and battleground rules regarding civilians. To Santa Anna, the slaughter at the Alamo and the massacres at Goliad would have been justified because they were a means to victory on a battlefield. He was, after all, conducting battle just a few decades after the end of the bloody Napoleonic Wars. When conducting a battle, Santa Anna was ruthless and did not apologize for it. The Texas Revolution came before the European movement for the nationalization of war, which means negotiating the release of prisoners in exchange for money was possible. However, it is unlikely that Santa Anna would have initially planned this for the civilians. According to conventional wisdom for a highly trained soldier, he would have interrogated them first.

Civilian prisoners would have been treated less harshly than any soldiers who were captured. Women, such as Emily, would have likely been with other New Washington residents. She may also have been kept with any women Santa Anna found at Harrisburg. The Mexican army would not have left them outside, where it would have been easier to escape. She would have been under guard in a camp tent, such as a headquarters tent.

Santa Anna did at times show marked civility toward women and children found on the battlefield. Susanna Dickinson claimed that after the Alamo, Santa Anna wanted her to come to Mexico with her infant. He promised them a life in a palace and that her child would be raised as an aristocrat. Another time, he adopted a white child, John C.C. Hill, and did exactly what he said he would do for Susanna's child. The general was introduced to the boy, who was at the Mier Expedition, in 1842. Santa Anna liked the twelve-year-old youngster with a big ego. He raised Hill as his own and gave him the title of a Mexican aristocrat. Hill returned to Texas throughout his life and considered himself an Anglo-Mexican. Santa Anna never made him deny his Anglo heritage. Emily's time as a prisoner may have been similar to what Hill and Dickinson experienced.

Like Dickinson and Hill, Emily and other civilian prisoners would have come before Santa Anna and other officers. By her own account, Emily had her free papers when she left the burned port. At her interrogation, any officer who spoke to her would have known she was an American citizen and not a Texas slave. While Santa Anna did not speak English, Almonte was fluent in United States customs, language and manners. He also had a respect for the Americans and knew how to interpret their ways, which Santa Anna found odd at times. Almonte would have been the most likely interpreter for Emily and others who were taken as prisoners. Also, Almonte spent time in the northeastern states where Emily was from. It wouldn't be farfetched to think he could have spoken to her about shared experiences or people they may have both known, such as Lundy.

Santa Anna may have wanted to know anything Emily and the prisoners knew about Burnet or de Zavala. The failed attempt to capture the Texas president and his mortal enemy was only compounded by the failed military tactics he was attempting. To end the rebellion, Santa Anna needed to capture the rebel government and quash the militia. Interrogation of any prisoners who worked at the war ports the rebels used would have been a necessity. He would have needed to know all he could about who was funding the rebels. He would have wanted to know the number of troops arriving at New Washington from America. He would have also wanted to know what kinds of ammunition and supplies were being shipped from New York through the ports. Anyone who knew anything about any of these matters would have been interrogated either by Santa Anna or one of his officers. The interviews would have been done within the days following their capture. The prisoners would have been separated and interrogated alone.

Whenever Santa Anna would have been present during a critical interrogation, it could have been conducted in his tent, where he could control access and ensure privacy. Other interrogations may have been in the headquarters tent. Emily probably knew something about almost every topic Santa Anna needed to know about. This means Santa Anna was probably very interested in Emily, especially when he realized she could read and write. Therefore, at some point during her seventy-two hours in the Mexican campground on the San Jacinto battleground, Emily probably was in a tent with Santa Anna.

No one will ever know if she told him a little or a lot.

Chapter 15

Fifteen Minutes and a Battle

April 21, 1836, was quiet until the afternoon, when General Martín Perfecto de Cos arrived with Mexican reinforcements over Vince's Bridge to Santa Anna's camp. His entrance lifted the troops' spirit, and they applauded his arrival with drums and cheers. The Mexican army swelled to 1,500 troops. Houston heard the arrival, and to stop any more reinforcements, he sent his spies to destroy the bridge. The decision meant Houston would leave Santa Anna without a retreat route. It also meant he and his men would not have one either.

But the Mexicans did not know Houston had done this at 9:00 a.m. As soon as the men arrived, Santa Anna acted as though it was a normal day. He ordered a *siesta*, said Delgado. "As it was represented to His Excellency that these men had not slept the night before, he instructed them to stack their arms, to remove their accoutrements, and to go to sleep quietly in the adjoining grove."

Santa Anna told his troops to rest on April 21 because he had no indication that the scruffy rebels would attack. Conventional European warfare called for an organized approach to the enemy. Battle lines were drawn, and then civility was issued before mass murder commenced. Texas had shown no sign of breaking these manners before San Jacinto. At the Alamo, Goliad and virtually every other prior engagement, the small band of Texans followed European warfare protocol. Travis responded with proper communication signals after Santa Anna made his intent known at the Alamo. Fannin issued his surrender at Goliad following the proper protocol. After their deaths, some Mexican officers remarked at the bravery Fannin and his troops showed upon defeat and death. Texans in every instance until San Jacinto had shown proper battlefield dignity. For the larger portion of the Texas Revolution, the rebels had fought like Europeans.

On the day of the Battle at San Jacinto, Santa Anna had no expectation that his camp, or post, would be subject to a surprise attack. It was unheard of before it happened. He may have thought the exchange, when it happened, would be brief and in his favor. Once he quashed the militia, he would move on to his grander vision. During the time he thought he had to prepare, he could have continued with the prisoner interrogations. In his tent, he could have had meetings with officers to decide their next moves. The troops could have had time with their camp followers, cleaned their weapons and other activities. They all could have rested, and even Santa Anna would have had a moment to relax in his tent.

The precursor activities to gentleman warfare ended when Houston gathered his men that morning and asked them if they wanted to attack the Mexican camp. James Washington Winters, a troop at the San Jacinto battle, remembered how the day transpired. He said Houston gathered a "council of war" before noon. He went to the troops' campfires as they ate a hefty breakfast for the first time in days. The night before, the troops had intercepted the flatboat that Santa Anna had filled days earlier with plundered flour and supplies from New Washington. The troops surmised Santa Anna was going to use the flatboat to move his men over the bayou. That didn't happen because the Texans kept the flatboat with its supplies and ate the food. The troops also had meat from the wild beeves they had slaughtered the day before. As they ate, Houston asked them personally if they wanted to attack Santa Anna. Winters said, "We replied with a shout that we were most anxious to do so. Then Houston replied, 'Very well, get your dinners and I will lead you into the fight, and if you whip them every one of you shall be a captain.'"

That afternoon, more than nine hundred men ate lunch and then lined themselves for battle. They were told that Def Smith had destroyed the bridge, and at 4:30 p.m., they began crawling up the earthen rise to attack. A single fife was playing "Will You Come to the Bower" as the fight song. The Irish tune is a political rally cry for those exiled from their country.

Delgado climbed on top of ammunition boxes to see that the Texans, with their flag in the center, were heading toward them in a full run. They had two cannons, and the cavalry was in front, overlapping their left. He said they were drunk and infuriated. Delgado was with Generals Manuel

Fernandez Castrillon and Almonte as they realized they were under a surprise attack.

> *At this fatal moment the bugler on our right signaled the advance of the enemy upon that wing. His Excellency and Staff were asleep; the greater number of the men were also sleeping; of the rest, some were eating, others were scattered in the woods in search of boughs to prepare shelter. Our line was composed of musket stacks. Our cavalry were riding bare-back to and from the water.*

According to Winters, some of the Mexican army were lying in the grass and began shooting as soon as he ran over the rise. It was the only defensive move the Mexicans ever made. After the battle was over, Winters said he returned to the grass and realized how few rounds were ever fired at them. "We examined the places where many had been, and found as many as five ends of cartridges where each Mexican lay, so supposed that each man had fired at us as many as five times before we reached them."

Upon attack, the Texans yelled, "Remember the Alamo!" and "Remember Goliad!" They reached the Mexicans at point-blank range, at which point they opened fire. Most of the Mexican officers were asleep when the Texans charged, leaving the camp followers and the troops in utter panic. General Castrillon realized what was happening. He got on his horse and attempted to rally the Mexican army out of the *siesta*. At his command, the army made a feeble attempt to engage, but they became confused, gave up and scattered when he was among the first killed. Winters remembered the moment the panic set in and he saw Castrillon fall as the slaughter began: "A Mexican officer tried to rally his men, but was soon dispatched by a rifle ball and fell from his horse. Our regiment passed beyond the Mexican's breastworks before we knew it, while our other two regiments came up in front of them, so then we did them up in short order."

Delgado's words confirm Winters's account. The Mexican troop said Mexico was so confused that eventually the Texans had control of an empty camp. The rebels ran to the center of the camp and quickly captured the artillery. Delgado said:

> *Then, already, I saw our men flying in small groups, terrified, and sheltering themselves behind large trees. I endeavored to force some of them to fight, but all efforts were in vain—the evil was beyond remedy; they were a bewildered and panic-stricken herd. The enemy kept up a brisk*

crossfire of grape on the woods. Presently we heard, in close proximity, the unpleasant noise of their clamors. Meeting no resistance, they dashed, lightning-like, upon our deserted camp.

Mexican troops, camp followers and Santa Anna's prisoners of war, like Emily, ran terrified over the marshes and prairies. The Mexican army began screaming that they were not at the Alamo or Goliad, but the Texans were in a sheer rage and followed them. The Texans began hand-to-hand combat and fired at the Mexicans until they had emptied their pistols. When they had no more bullets, they began using their guns as clubs. When they had no clubs, they used knives to slaughter and stab the Mexican troops. When they had no knives, they drove the Mexicans into the bayou and drowned them.

In conventional battle terms, the Texans won the battle within minutes, but the victory didn't stop the overkill. Houston had no control over the troops. The battle was a bloody, savage event that didn't stop until nightfall. Winters remembered how the troops kept pursuing every Mexican troop:

I never heard any halt ordered. We never halted. The battle was won in fifteen or eighteen minutes. The Mexican cavalry broke in disorder, while ours was hotly pursuing them. Houston had two horses killed from under him, and was on his third one before he passed the Mexican's [sic] works. We ran and fought fully two miles.

So many Mexicans were killed that their dead bodies and horses made a bridge across the bayou. The waters and campground were blood-red. None of the Texas leaders could control the slaughter, Winters remembered.

General Wharton tried to get us to cease and grabbed a Mexican and pulled him up behind him on his horse, saying that was his Mexican, but Jim Curtis shot the Mexican. The Mexican infantry near the lake would jump in occasionally and would dive to get away from our shots, but the minute they would raise their heads they were picked off by our men.

As a result, some Mexicans ran to Vince's Bridge. Seeing it was destroyed, they got on their horses and tried to ride down the steep bank. Others dismounted and began trying to swim in the swollen and rushing bayou. In response, the Texans poured a fire on them and left them to die by fire or flood. Winters remembered the death trap and what happened to those who didn't burn or drown: "Only a few followed the flying Mexicans to Vince's bayou; the Mexicans finding the bridge burned, tried to cross, but their horses bogged. Only one of those trying to cross there got away all the others were shot."

After the slaughter ended, Houston still had no control of the troops, according to Winters:

> *After the fight was ended Houston gave orders to form in line and march back to camp, but we payed no attention to him, as we were all shaking hands and rejoicing over the victory. Houston gave the order three times and still the men payed no attention to him. And he turned his horse around and said "Men, I can gain victories with you, but damn your manners" and rode on to camp.*

In the end, 630 Mexican troops died, 208 were wounded and 730 were taken prisoner. Santa Anna ran and was captured the next day. He surrendered to Houston.

Emily experienced ravage abolitionist riots in New York that lasted for days upon days only to survive the overkill horror of a fifteen-minute Texas victory. Her battle, however, had just begun.

The Battle of San Jacinto. *Courtesy of Henry Arthur McArdle.*

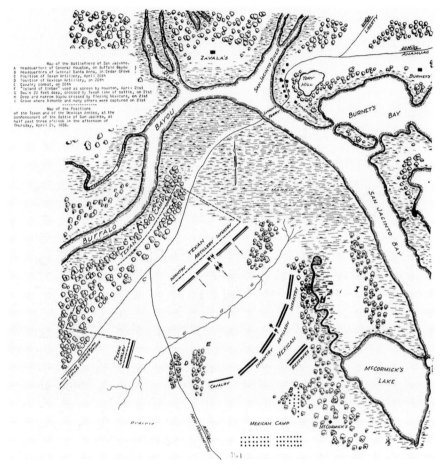

Above: Drawn in 1837, this map shows troop movements in the Battle of San Jacinto. *Courtesy of Anson Jones Press.*

Opposite, top: The San Jacinto battlefield site with NASA jet flyover in 1998. *Courtesy of NASA.*

Opposite, bottom: NASA jets fly over the San Jacinto battlefield and Houston Ship Channel in 1998. *Courtesy of NASA.*

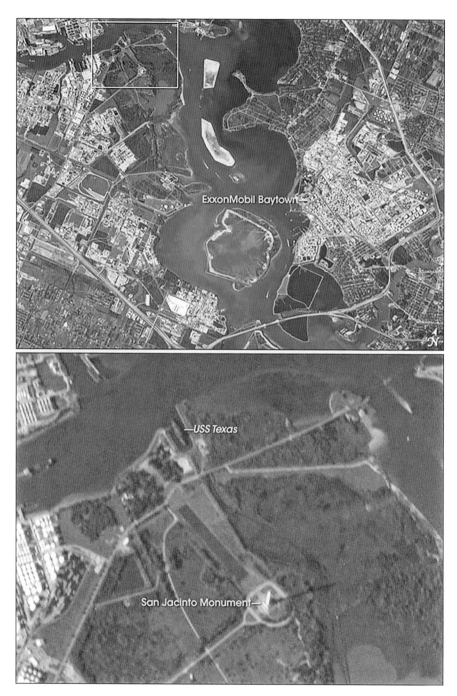

A map, circa 1998, that shows the modern-day locations of the Houston Ship Channel and the San Jacinto Monument. *Courtesy of NASA.*

116

San Jacinto Memorial Monument and Museum, Houston, Texas

SEE OTHER SIDE

An early twentieth-century postcard of the San Jacinto Monument. *Courtesy of Morse Wholesale, Houston, Texas.*

Chapter 16

Paperless

The state of the frenzied Texans brought utter fear to a veteran Mexican war general. When Santa Anna was captured the following day, some troops demanded that Houston kill him. Houston thought differently. Their fury and the horror of the previous forty-eight hours had scared General Cos so much that he huddled in fear. Winters said, "I do not know who captured Cos, but he was the most frightened man I ever saw. He covered his head with a blanket. I could see it tremble twenty feet off."

As the days continued, it became obvious that Houston was not going to order the execution of Santa Anna or anyone else. In fact, he sent away the troops who demanded execution. He allowed the general to retrieve his tent and most of its contents. Houston also let Santa Anna sleep on his own cot in his tent while he slept on the ground with the Texans. Houston's gentlemanly conduct continued for weeks as the Texan negotiated the independence of Texas. In the days after the battle, with the corpses of the Mexican soldiers still on the field, Houston said he put Sydney Sherman in charge of the spoils. Sherman ordered that any money or valuables found on the dead be brought back to camp for collection. The troops gathered supplies, livestock, belongings and other spoils. Winters followed Sherman's instructions. He said, "I found a dead Mexican who had silver in his belt—about ten dollars. The money had slipped out when he was shot. Orders were given that all money found be brought into headquarters. I turned this in."

Soon the stench of the rotting corpses became too strong, and the camp moved to the plantation of George Patrick, who worked with Morgan at New Washington. Winters recalls what Houston did with the money found on the battlefield: "Money so captured was distributed to the soldiers, the amount so distributed averaging almost $11 per man."

About 12,000 pesos were collected from the Mexican bodies and divided among the troops. The men then began auctioning off the spoils. Muskets, saddles, blankets, spurs, horses and mules were among the items purchased. Some of Santa Anna's own belongings were also auctioned. Winters remembered how they bought gifts for Houston: "Santa Anna's handsomely ornamented saddle was held up and the men voted that it should be given to General Houston. Other officers' saddles were sold. One brought as high as $300."

The troops also bought Santa Anna's chamber pot and gave it to Houston, probably as a joke. It was a gift that embarrassed him for the rest of his life, and he never left any written documentation that he owned it. The camp followers and prisoners of war were also at the Texas camp and eventually released.

Emily, however, was in a vulnerable position. She had lost her free papers in the fury of the battle. To make matters worse, the day after the battle, the Texans set fire to the prairie. Winters said it was to force other Mexican troops from hiding. Delgado said it was because Texans were playing with gunpowder and lost control of it. Regardless of why it was lit, her chances of finding her passport were remote. By law, if she was not able to convince the Texans that she was a free person of color who had immigrated in 1835, she would be considered a slave and sold. She must have pleaded her case well. Houston and his militia recognized her status, and she was released.

The independence of Texas changed other important factors for free blacks. It also created a shift in relations between the abolitionists in New York and the burgeoning republic. Lundy had an agreement with the Mexican government to build a free black colony in Texas. He did not have an agreement with the new republic. It would have been well known that Houston was negotiating Texas's freedom with Santa Anna so the territory could become a new slave republic. In fact, the new government was quick to legalize chattel slavery to quash any river plantation fears that the new leaders would follow any bit of Mexico's antislavery sentiments. The new leaders maintained general provisions that also made sure no slave could be given freedom. Even Congress would not be allowed to grant manumission.

With the issue of slavery settled, many early Texans turned their attention to another fear. They were distrustful of free blacks. At the outbreak of the revolution, a Beaumont committee on safety asked for legislation that would record free blacks in a designated citizen class. The committee wanted free blacks in a category distinct from whites and slaves. The committee also asked the General Council to prevent the immigration of free blacks and mixed-race people into Texas. While Emily was a free black, it was clear that her equal status under Texas law was not secure.

At its core, the Beaumont letter addressed the fear that free blacks might incite thoughts of freedom in a slave. About one hundred slaves staged an uprising on the Brazos River at the dawn of the revolution, which plantation owners quickly quashed. The slaves were either "whipped nearly to death, some hung, etc.," according to Major Sutherland as he reported the news to the troops at Goliad. He had come to gather a few of them to help maintain order after the event. The images of insurrections, such as the Nat Turner Rebellion, still lingered in the minds of most white people. Plantation owners did not want to see a slave uprising repeated in their river towns. The possibility of Lundy's colony contract may have also frightened them. They alluded to such a possibility when they wrote:

> *The resident of such free Negroes and mulattoes among us, would prove an evil difficult to be remedied should it once be tolerated. To the slaveholder nothing could be of deeper interest than the timely adoption of some measures that will prove effectually preventive of a course so much to be dreaded in a country whose soil, from the nature of its productions must be cultivated by slave labor.*

News spread slowly in the dawn of the Texas Revolution, but at some point during her stay, Emily would have learned that on January 5, 1836—just weeks after her arrival—the General Council passed a decree that prevented the importation or immigration of free blacks and mixed-race people into Texas. Given that Texas secured its independence from Mexico, she would have realized that Lundy's dream of a free black colony was not going to happen. The decree also stated that should a free black enter the territory, he or she would be sold on the auction block.

To make matters worse, the rebel government deputized every settler and offered one-third of the proceeds of the slave sale to the arresting citizen. Even if Emily could prove she was a free black, she now had to prove she had immigrated before the law took effect. Unscrupulous Texas settlers had been given a government-sponsored financial incentive to make sure she didn't. Without her free papers, she couldn't prove anything. At any moment, she could be made a slave.

Emily lived under this cloud for more than a year and was still able to maintain her free black status. On June 5, 1837, Congress passed another decree that addressed the status of free blacks. A joint resolution upheld their equal status under the law, if they followed all the provisions the government required of them. By this time, however, Emily was actively seeking someone to vouch for her status so she could receive a passport and leave Texas. By returning to New York, her status as a free black woman would be secure because the state granted it to her as either her birthright or as a matter of law.

In the early republic, if a person wanted a passport, he or she would simply write a letter to the State Department. The letter was reviewed, and an official wrote a letter that served as a passport. It may contain the places a person might want to travel. Houston had a passport that listed European countries he never visited. Others might contain what the person looked like. The letter was essentially a permission slip that allowed a person to travel in and out of Texas. It included a hand-drawn seal, since the new republic had no real stationery.

When Emily decided to return to New York in 1837, she attempted to get a passport from the secretary of state, Robert Irion. Houston appointed Irion to the position for one year, and he traveled extensively while in the post. He was a trained and educated physician. He did not serve as a troop in the revolution, although he was an active politician and legislator. Irion did not give Emily her passport easily. He wanted someone to verify her story.

She asked Issac Moreland, a veteran of the Battle at San Jacinto, to write a letter on her behalf, and he agreed to do so. Moreland was a strategic choice because by this time, her boss, Morgan, was having disagreements with Houston. Moreland, on the other hand, had positive relationships throughout Texas. He received a certificate of character in 1834 from Judge William Hardin, which meant that the judge had vouched for his honesty and integrity to the Mexican government. Moreland was also one of the first Texas Masons. According to Dr. Labadie, who was present with Moreland at the pre-revolution Liberty Convention, Moreland was able to inspire and arouse the crowd through his thrilling storytelling. As the revolution peaked, the rebel government named Moreland captain of the artillery. It was a position he would keep for some time. In that role, he commanded the Twin Sisters cannon crew during the San Jacinto battle. A month before he vouched for Emily, he opened a law office with Burnet to serve settlers in Liberty and Harrisburg. It was after the battle, probably when the Texans were processing Santa Anna's prisoners, that he met Emily. He also kept in touch with her while he was the postmaster in Galveston during the dawn of the republic. In his letter to Irion, which contains the date July 1837, he wrote:

> *Capitol, Thursday Morning*
> *To the Hon. Dr. Irion*
> *The bearer of this—Emily D. West has been since my first acquaintance with her, in April of –36 a free woman—she Emigrated to this Country with Col. Ja's Morgan from the state of N. York in September of 35 and is now anxious to return and wishes a passport—I believe myself, that she is entitled to one and has requested me to give her this note to you.*
>
> *Your Obd't Serv't*
> *I.N. Moreland*

Around his signature, he wrote an additional note, which he signed with his name. Given that the statement was an add-on, Emily might have asked him to write the line to prove to Irion that she lost her papers on the battlefield. Moreland wrote:

> *Her free papers were Lost at San Jacinto as I am Informed and believe in April of –36*
> *Moreland*

Texas then loses track of Emily. Conventional wisdom maintains that she returned to New York. It's unknown if she ever received payment from Morgan or if she maintained a relationship with any of those she worked with. Little is known about the prisoners Santa Anna took from Harrisburg and New Washington. How she survived after the revolution also remains unknown. Morgan never rebuilt the port and, instead, built a town under the name of the New Washington Association's prime investor, Samuel Swartwout. It's unknown if she worked there. Something incredible had to have surrounded Emily's situation in Texas for her to keep her free status without her papers. She had to have had protection for more than a year, but it's unknown who gave it to her and how she survived through that year and three months.

It also remains unknown if Lundy, Jocelyn or the Tappan brothers ever knew about Emily's vulnerable predicament and if they intervened or tried to help her. In all actuality, it remains unclear if she ever got the passport at all, although the chances are high that she did since Moreland was well respected. What does remain clear about her story is that Emily, a single, free black woman, had her own war to win after the Texas Revolution.

She fought to maintain her rights under a system that wanted to chip them away until she had none.

Chapter 17

Houston and Emily

I n the years after the Texas Revolution, English travelers would explore the new republic. Travelers were not unique in the 1800s and acted like international public information specialists, journalists and public fact-gatherers. They had access, usually, to high-level leaders and roamed freely among the settlers and sometimes the government. Almonte was a traveler for the Mexican government in the United States. He acquired so much great knowledge about the United States and its people that Santa Anna relied on him to decipher the ways of the Texan militia. John Poinset was a United States traveler who went many places, including Russia and Mexico. While on one of his Central and South American travels, he discovered a beautiful flowering bush. When he brought it back to America, the bush was named after him. It became known as the poinsettia.

These traveler's diaries and journals resembled the work of a modern reporter or researcher notebook. Some of the information they contained was considered very reliable and therefore became part of the traveler's official account to the government. Other pieces were recorded for other reasons. Some of the information, just like a reporter's notebook, contained information that was recorded but may not have been intended for publication or public consumption. In other words, the traveler might keep the entry but essentially considered it tossed for any number of reasons.

England was in favor of Texas becoming a nation that could supply it with cash crops. It favored the revolution, and in order to access possible opportunities, it sent a battery of travelers to write about the land. William

Bollaert was one of these government-sponsored travelers. Bollaert was a trained and educated man who worked as a writer, chemist, geographer and ethnologist. As such, most of his reports focused on geography, climate, natural resources and demographics. He traveled to Peru and Portugal before he came to Texas, and many scientists held his observations in high regard. He arrived in Texas in 1842 to create a report for the British admiralty. On his visit, he was commissioned to study the land west of San Antonio to see if it could be colonized with British immigrants. His published works on Texas included a support of slavery. He did not believe enough whites could be hired to work the fields, so he supported chattel slavery as an economic foundation for Texas.

He had two chief sources for his reports: Houston, who became the first president of the Republic of Texas following his victory at San Jacinto, and Mirabeau B. Lamar, who was the republic's second president. At the end of Bollaert's journey, the bulk of his observations were about the areas he was trained in. In addition to his commissioned report, he later wrote a handful of reports about Texas after it was annexed. They were published in popular English journals. Some were published anonymously. He also had long lists of notes and private pieces. It's unclear what he wanted to do with them, but they were not used in any other works. Maybe he wanted to publish them later, or maybe he wanted to use them for something else. Either way, they were personal. He organized them into a "Texas Manuscript" that contained six diaries and two volumes of journals.

Inside this oeuvre are two pieces he never used or published. One of them he wanted to keep so private that he underlined the word "private" three times. This was a seemingly random letter that Sam Houston wrote to someone else. It reads:

> *The Battle of San Jacinto was probably lost to the Mexicans, owing to the influence of a Mulatta girl* [Emily] *belonging to Col. Morgan who was closeted in the tent with g'l Santana, at the time the cry was made, "The Enemy! They come! They come!" and detained Santana so long, that order could not be restored readily again.*

The other entry is an essay Bollaert wrote about Emily that builds on Houston's words. Bollaert's source was described as an "officer who was at the battle." This essay claims Emily was having sex with Santa Anna during the siesta so Houston could launch his surprise attack. In other words, she supported the Texas rebels as a covert sex spy.

Over the years, an audience grew that claimed Houston's letter reveals important undiscovered information about the battle and Houston was the source for Bollaert's essay. If Houston did mean the words Bollaert wrote, then the Texan was deliberately belittling his own accomplishments at San Jacinto. They were accomplishments that he spent most of his life defending because he was a consistently controversial figure. Years after Bollaert left Texas, Houston gave a lengthy exhaustive speech to vindicate himself as a military hero to the U.S. Senate. On February 28, 1859, Houston doesn't mention any woman having sex with Santa Anna in a tent when Texas troops attack at San Jacinto. Instead, he recounts the strategic decisions he made in deep detail and explains clearly how his troops devised a surprise attack on Santa Anna. According to his official testimony, while his men suggested unconventional means to warfare, they did not mention the use of a sexual seductress. Houston said, "The proposition was put to the council, 'shall we attack the enemy in position, or receive their attack in ours?' The two junior officers—for such is the way of taking the sense of courts in the army—were in favor of attacking the enemy in position."

Then Houston stated that the senior officers told him they could stage an attack that never had been done before. Their method essentially dispensed with proper European war conduct. He said, "The four seniors and the Secretary of War who spoke said that 'to attack veteran troops with raw militia is a thing unheard of; to charge upon the enemy without bayonets in an open prairie had never been known; our situation is strong; in it we can whip all of Mexico.'"

The troops' words, as recounted by Houston, make it clear they didn't need help winning the battle from a free black woman never trained in military action because they were going to launch a guerrilla attack. Houston certainly would have known Emily's truth. He would have heard her story post-battle and learned that she was a free black woman employed at the port. He would have known she lost her free papers on the battlefield and that she was not married. If Houston told Bollaert the story and/or if he wrote the words in a letter as an underreported military strategy, then a Texas hero deliberately chose to portray a free black woman as a slave.

By the time Bollaert met Houston, however, there could have been reason to sully a free black woman's reputation, especially if she was single and with no family to defend her. In 1840, two years before Bollaert arrived in Texas, the legislature stripped free blacks of their citizenship. The new republic gave them eighteen months to leave the state or be sold as slaves on the auction block. The Englishman arrived at a pivotal Texas moment when any free black still in Texas was being forced into chattel slavery or was fleeing the republic for his or her freedom. The sentiment that free blacks were a threat to the slave economy was still very real. Texas was quickly moving from a state with slaves to a slave state.

During this time, several stereotypes were used to justify slavery. These characterizations heightened distrust of free blacks and demoralized African Americans in the eyes of whites. One was the hypersexualized black man and woman. The New Washington Association investor, the publisher James Webb, used this tactic when he was creating fake news accounts about free blacks in New York in order to incite strings of riots. His earliest account of this was the "dandys" riding their horses along Broadway. "Dandy" was a term that exaggerated a well-dressed, mannered, highbrow, educated free black. It was one of two major characters featured in minstrel skits. The other was the happy, silly, plantation-loving slave.

In other words, the Texas mindset in the 1840s may have influenced the creation of a highly sexualized, unsubstantiated tale of a free, educated black woman who probably never knew it was being told. If Emily was a sex spy for Texas, she was sacrificing herself for a rebel government that she knew at some point would never support a colony of her people. As a spy, she probably wouldn't have wanted to leave the republic she fought for even if it whittled away her personal rights. What she actually did stands in direct contradiction to the tale. Moreland wrote to Irion that Emily told him she was *anxious* to leave Texas and return to New York.

Another reason that Houston may have been willing to concoct a sexual account about Emily would have been to belittle Santa Anna, who claimed he was under a tree when Houston attacked. Houston was in a popularity contest to secure his legacy in post-revolution Texas. According to veteran Winters, Santa Anna wasn't the only general who couldn't control his troops on the battlefield that day. Houston couldn't get his men to reform after the vicious battle either. Eventually, he gave up and rode off without them. The story could have been a ruse to take the sting off any criticism about Houston, which he was aware was growing. In 1842, Houston was in a political wrangle to move the Texas capital and the republic archives from Austin to the town named after him. The fight was known as the Texas Archive War, and sentiment against him was so bitter that his own private secretary told him the people would rather fight him than the Mexicans. A fable about a Texas seductress creates a narrative that Santa Anna was a poor general who preferred sex over duty and then ran away and hid like a coward during battle. Houston looks like a hero.

According to Santa Anna's own staff, both sides have plenty of reason to belittle the general. The choice for the campground was terrible, Delgado said. He noticed right away that they were pinned and that Texas was in a better position to attack. He complained, "The camping-ground of His Excellency's selection was, in all respects, against military rules. Any youngster would have done better."

At the time of the Texas attack, Delgado was on guard with Generals Castrillon and Almonte. Delgado saw what he called an "extended line that was well manned" descending on them. Neither general at the time was able to control the troops, and confusion began almost immediately. When Santa Anna came out of his tent, he was running around in excitement, wringing his hands and so overwhelmed that he gave no orders. Delgado described how the general had what could be considered a meltdown:

> *To this disposition, yelling furiously, with a brisk fire of grape, muskets, and rifles, they* [Texas] *advanced resolutely upon our camp. There the utmost confusion prevailed. General Castrillon shouted on one side; on another Colonel Almonte was giving orders; some cried out to commence firing; others to lie down to avoid grape-shots. Among the latter was His Excellency.*

Delgado does not mention once that Santa Anna lost focus on the battle because he was having sex with an American in his tent. He lost focus, according to Delgado, because he was a bad general.

THE BATTLE OF THE TRAVELERS

When Bollaert returned to England, a flurry of travelers had already published a wide array of opinions about Texas. The topic of the faraway land was popular with readers, and they were enthralled with the territory and its people. Texas topics ranged from gossip to humor to cultural commentary to political analysis. Their work was so widely read that travelers would publicly debate their work and research, much like media commentators. Some travelers, like Bollaert, thought highly of Texas people and its leadership. Some did not. Harriett Martineau charged the Texans with committing the most highhanded theft in modern times. She was among those who wrote favorably about Mexico and thought the

Texas rebels had committed treason. She was one that Lundy might have liked to read.

Travelers were also divided over annexation. Some wrote articles that claimed the United States didn't want another slave state and Texas would be its own nation. Travelers also argued over the Texas people and culture. When N. Doran Maillard, an abolitionist, wrote about horrible Texan customs, including the women who smoked pipes and used snuff, Bollaert came to the defense of Texas women. He claimed the fellow traveler had never been introduced to its society of ladies and had never been subjected to the hospitable kindness of its river plantation owners.

Bollaert wrote a total of eighty articles for a wide array of English journals. He completed three books. He published ten articles about Texas. Not one of them contained the sexualized account of Emily West as a free black woman or a slave. Until he died in 1867, his tale and the random Houston letter remained unpublished for reasons he never revealed and have still never been uncovered.

Chapter 18

Fake News Rises and Falls

In 1902, after Bollaert died, Edward E. Ayer bought the "Texas Manuscript" from the traveler's family and later gifted the oeuvre to the Chicago Newberry Library. For almost half a decade, the salacious fable about Emily languished in the archives.

Meanwhile, the "Yellow Rose of Texas" song began a new life. After it was sung by Confederates in the Civil War, it was reinvigorated during the Depression. In 1936, the racist lyrics were sanitized for the Texas Centennial celebration. The decision launched the state's unofficial anthem. As the song's popularity rose, the new version became commercialized and was used to sell Texas as a prosperous land with a larger-than-life culture. The song sold everything from politicians to Texas-made sliced bread and the high school Friday night football culture.

In 1948, a dozen years after the song embedded itself into mainstream Texas culture, Bollaert's sexualized tale about Emily was found in the archives. A University of Texas department chair, Joe Frantz, referenced the unpublished narrative in his doctoral dissertation. His footnote did not move the story into the mainstream, however. The sexual tale also didn't capture general public fancy in 1951 when it was included in the biography of Gail Borden, the founder of Borden's Milk. Meanwhile, in 1955, Mitch Miller's rendition of "The Yellow Rose of Texas" became one of the most popular tunes in the world, and girls were being crowned in its name. While the world whistled the catchy tune, it still wasn't linked to Bollaert's tale.

Tale and song still didn't merge when two academics gathered the "Texas Manuscript" in the Newberry archives and began translating the handwritten pages into a mainstream book. They selected pieces of Bollaert's published and unpublished writings. Eugene Hollon and Ruth Lapham Butler hoped the book, *William Bollaert's Texas*, would become a seminal work on Texas history and culture. They chose to include the story about Emily as a sexual femme fatale as a footnote, which can be found on page 108 of the published book. Hollon worked at the University of Oklahoma, and Butler was a Newberry custodian in charge of the "Texas Manuscript" and Ayer's gift.

The process to publication was not smooth. While the two academics chose manuscripts for the book, Hollon's curating techniques received criticism from the Newberry director, Stanley Pargellis. On September 20, 1955, the university's publisher, Savoie Lottinville, wrote to him in hopes of calming the disagreement:

> *I can't tell you how sorry I am about the Hollon matter. I called him today to ask him about his interpretations, and he said that there were frequently two or three, even more, entries for a given day, and that he chose the one which seemed to him best to represent Bollaert's thinking at the time. Even so, I can't understand how he missed—or appeared to miss—so completely certain types of expression. This may not be attributed to unfamiliarity with English idiom, in my opinion, but may trace to a certain blindness in orthography and vocabulary command which is all too common among young scholars today, but really is not characteristic of men of his age and time.*
>
> *If we can straighten out the problem down here, I would be quite prepared to attempt it, because I don't like to think of your being occupied with a task as long drawn out and as needless as this one. But you must be best judge.*

Despite the issues, Pargellis eventually wrote the book's foreword, and it became the seminal work Hollon and Butler wanted it to be. Butler was lauded for the mark she put on the collection and her interpretation of it. The book caught the imagination of a divided nation that was struggling to come to terms with a new slate of racial issues. The nation had put an end to the Jim Crow era, named after the character the minstrels promoted. Two years before the book's publication, the United States Supreme Court reversed the 1896 *Plessy v. Ferguson* opinion that codified the Jim Crow laws. The nation was also reeling from a court's ruling that desegregated public schools. The case was called *Brown v. Board of Education of Topeka*. The United States was at the dawn of the civil rights era and looking for stories that exalted national pride as it moved squarely into the Cold War. *William Bollaert's Texas* provided comfort for all the issues the nation had on its plate.

A LEGEND IS BORN

In 1961, a journalist became a Bollaert fan after he read Hollon's book. Henderson Shuffler was enthralled with the tale of Emily West and believed it. He was smitten with the idea that she hadn't gotten the glory she deserved for her grand sexual sacrifice. He worked at the University of Texas A&M, and at one point, he was invited to speak at the San Jacinto Monument, which was erected to memorialize the battle. During his speech, he broached the idea that Emily West was the Yellow Rose of Texas. Once the song and the woman were connected, a legend was conceived. Like the minstrels, who believed they were celebrating blacks in their stage portrayals, Shuffler believed he was elevating Emily by connecting her to a minstrel song.

Shuffler began pushing his tale and told it to another journalist, Frank Tolbert. Tolbert worked for the *Dallas Morning News* and was one of the state's most popular reporters. He was also well respected within his profession. Tolbert repeated Shuffler's assertions with gusto and promoted the connection between the woman and the song. If Shuffler concocted the legend, Tolbert embedded it into Texas culture. Between Tolbert and Shuffler, the story grew until Emily became a celebrated cartoon. While no one can document what she looked like, they gave her "Latin-like" features and described her as beautiful. They created an elaborate fantasy about her using the hypersexualized African American stereotype. Tolbert said her walk was the most exciting thing about New Washington. At another point, Tolbert suggested that the state place a stone on the San Jacinto battleground "In Honor of Emily Who Gave Her All for Texas Piece by Piece." The monument administration and board thought better of the idea.

In 1976, as women were fighting for the Equal Rights Amendment, Martha Turner, an English academic at Sam Houston State University, added to the gender and race exploitation with a fictional book, *The Yellow Rose of Texas: Her Saga and Her Song.* It built on Tolbert's themes and added more fantasy to Emily's story. By 1986, journalists throughout Texas were in a frenzy about the beautiful sexual woman named Emily West and spread the fable during the Texas Sesquicentennial Celebration.

A secret all-male society called the Sons of the Knights of the Yellow Rose met with the single mission to concoct more myths about Emily. One was that she roamed the San Jacinto Battlefield as a ghost. If a person walked the battlefield at night but didn't see her, she was walking somewhere else. It certainly was not because she wasn't there.

When the media, Hollywood, academia and a group of Texas men finished with her reputation, Emily was Santa Anna's lover and deserved credit for her sexual abilities. When that appropriation still wasn't enough, they began adding fables that she sent messages to Houston about what Santa Anna was doing and other movements that Houston needed to know about Mexico's position.

By the time the 1980s arrived, Emily's experience as a prisoner of war and her efforts to rebuild her life as a free black woman in Texas were lost forever. When James Michener brings up Emily in his novel *Texas*, she wasn't even a spy who used seduction as a war tool anymore. She was a common whore who wanted Santa Anna as a notch on her belt. In San Antonio, a place she never visited, a hotel was named after her based on the legend. The Emily Morgan hotel, across the street from the Alamo, is formally named Emily West Morgan, but it uses her misappropriated slave name for marketing. The legend is cherished throughout its branding plan. In Houston, Veryl Goodnight, a sculptor, created a statue of Emily, a woman whose features and physical description were never recorded.

As the latter century moved into the new millennium, the United States' affair with national mythmaking began to subside. As that happened, Emily's appropriated story melted so deep into Texas lore that it couldn't be distinguished among the song, the legend and her actual biography, albeit scant. As the nation moved further into the twenty-first century, the fable and song began to be studied through a new lens that questioned why the story had only been told through one interpretation that relied completely on Bollaert's oeuvre. Previous generations, however, had planted seeds that they, too, were skeptical of the legend and those who were part of it.

In the town of Morgan's Point at the original New Washington Association port, city leaders made the Yellow Rose of Texas the centerpiece of the town's story. It is also the city logo. Long after Morgan was gone, city leaders agreed to give up a good chunk of the town so the Port of Houston could be built. Along its interior miles of port containers, ships and cranes overlook the community and the town cemetery where James Morgan was buried. City workers have surrounded his tombstone with a barrier decorated with Yellow Rose logos and the Lone Star emblem.

The logo of the City of Morgan's Point includes the Yellow Rose of Texas. *Author's photo.*

James Morgan's grave site is surrounded by a barrier fence donned with the Lone Star emblem and the Yellow Rose of Texas. *Author's photo.*

Morgan might be the namesake; however, Emily is the rose. Yellow roses don the entrance to the town. Symbols of the rose are featured on city facilities. During the Texas Sesquicentennial, the Beta Sigma Phi sorority placed a kiosk about Emily's legend at the front of the cemetery. The kiosk blatantly dismissed the dalliance with Santa Anna but paid homage to what was known about her true biography at the time. For decades, another kiosk was also at the front of the cemetery that was not placed there by the sorority. It was removed during the past decade. The removed kiosk contained a narrative that teased the visitor, or mourner, into thinking that Emily might be buried at the cemetery with Morgan. Even during the peak of the legend's popularity, women in the community could distinguish among a media-fueled fable, the woman, the Bollaert tale and the song.

Even as the male-dominated narrative of Emily's story gained hold in mainstream Texas, another group of men simultaneously began to reshape the Yellow Rose symbol as a celebration of female strength and civic courage. In 1950s, Texas governor Allan Shivers began the

The Beta Sigma Phi sorority placed a marker during the Texas Sesquicentennial at the entrance of the city of Morgan's Point Cemetery. *Author's photo.*

The gateway to Morgan's Point, which was the original site of New Washington Association, features the Yellow Rose of Texas logo. *Author's photo.*

Commission of the Yellow Rose, commonly known as the Yellow Rose of Texas Award. Over the decades, it has honored women who exhibited outstanding community service or made significant efforts to preserve Texas history. The award predated the legend, although some news stories as late as 2012 state that it was created to celebrate the Tolbert-Shuffler fabrications. These millennial news stories illustrate how deeply ingrained Emily has become in Texas culture. They also reveal how deep the confusion about her true story and the fake news surrounding it has become. The strong, single free black woman who survived abolitionist riots and a rebel revolution on her own terms has become exactly what late-century mythmakers wanted her to be. Emily has become a ghost that Texans understand in glimpses but never see in clear focus.

She didn't give herself up piece by piece, but over the centuries, she has survived that way.

Above: The City of Morgan's Point Cemetery sits in the center of the Port of Houston as the oldest municipal cemetery in Harris County. *Author's photo*.

Left: The entrance to Morgan's Point Cemetery, where James Morgan is buried. *Author's photo*.

What is known today as the Houston Ship Channel was the waterway from New Washington Association to Galveston during the Texas Revolution. *Author's photo.*

Decades before the Houston Ship Channel became the waterway for the Houston Port, it was the site of the Battle of San Jacinto. *Author's photo.*

Bibliography

Books

Barker, Eugene C., Charles Shirley Potts and Charles W. Ramsdell. *A School History of Texas*. Chicago: Row, Peterson & Company, 1912.

Bean, AnneMarie, James V. Hatch and Brooks McNamera, eds. *Inside the Minstrel Mask: Readings in Nineteenth-Century Blackface Minstrelsy*. 1st ed. Middletown, CT: Wesleyan University Press, 1996.

Burrows, Edwin G., and Mike Wallace. *Gotham: A History of New York City to 1898*. Oxford, UK: Oxford University Press, 1999.

Caplan, Colin M. *Legendary Locals of New Haven*. Charleston, SC: Arcadia Publishing, 2013.

Crane, William Carey, Rod Oliver and Sam Houston. *Life and Select Literary Remains of Sam Houston, of Texas: Two Vols. in One*. Philadelphia: J.P. Lippincott & Co., 1884.

Crockett, D., A.J. Dumas and C.T. Beale. *Life of David Crockett, the Original Humorist and Irrepressible Backwoodsman: Comprising His Early History; His Bear-Hunting and Other Adventures; His Services in the Creek War; His Electioneering Speeches and Career in Congress; with His Triumphal Tour through the Northern States, and Services in the Texas War. To Which Is Added an Account of His Glorious Death at the Alamo While Fighting in Defence of Texan Independence*. Philadelphia: J.E. Potter, 1865.

The Five Points Mission. *The Old Brewery, and the New Mission House at the Five Points*. New York: Stringer & Townsend, 1854.

Galveston News. *The Texas Almanac for 1857.* Galveston, TX: Richardson, 1856.

Garrison, Wendell Phillips. *Williams Lloyd Garrison, 1805–1879: The Story of His Life as Told by His Children.* New York: Century, 1855.

Groneman, William. *David Crockett: Hero of the Common Man (American Heroes).* New York: Forge Books, 2005.

Hart, Albert Bushnell. "Slavery and Abolition 1831–1841." *The American National: A History.* N.p., 1906.

Headley, J.T. *The Great Riots of New York, 1712 to 1873.* Charleston, SC: BiblioBazaar, 2006.

Kemp, L.W., and Ed Kilman. *The Battle of San Jacinto and the San Jacinto Campaign.* Houston: Webb Printing, 1947.

Lester, Charles Edwards. *The Life of Sam Houston: The Hunter, Patriot, and Statesman of Texas.* Philadelphia: G.G. Evans, 1860.

———. *The Life of Sam Houston: The Only Authentic Memoir of Him Ever Published.* New York: J.C. Derby, 1899.

Lundy, Benjamin. *The War in Texas; a Review of Facts and Circumstances, Showing That This Contest Is a Crusade against Mexico, Set on Foot by Slaveholders, Land Speculators, & C. in Order to Re-establish, Extend, and Perpetuate the System of Slavery and the Slave Trade.* 2nd ed. Philadelphia: Merrihew and Gunn, 1837.

Mates, Julian. *America's Musical Stage: Two Hundred Years of Musical Theatre.* West Port, CT: Praeger, 1985.

Newman, Richard S., and James Mueller. *Antislavery and Abolition in Philadelphia.* Baton Rouge: Louisiana State University Press, 2011.

Steele, Alfonso. *Biography of Private Alfonso Steele, Only Survivor of the Battle of San Jacinto, Together with Mr. Steele's Account of the Campaign and Fight, and the Official Report of Gen. Sam Houston, with Complete Roster of the Commands Composing the Little Army.* Internet Archive. Accessed December 18, 2018.

Tappan, Lewis. *The Life of Arthur Tappan.* New York: Hurd & Houghton, 1870.

Tucker, Phillip Thomas. *Emily D. West and the "Yellow Rose of Texas" Myth.* Jefferson, NC: McFarland & Company, 2014.

Wooten, Dudley Goodall. *A Complete History of Texas for Schools, Colleges and General Use.* Dallas: Texas History Company, 1899.

Encyclopedia and Archives

"Jim Crow Law History & Facts." 2019. Encyclopedia Britannica. www.britannica.com/event/Jim-Crow-law.

"Minstrel Show Description, History, & Facts." Encyclopedia Britannica. January 16, 2019. www.britannica.com/art/minstrel-show.

"Newberry Digital Exhibitions Realizing the Newberry Idea, 1887–2012: Scholar-Librarians: Pierce and Ruth Lapham Butler." 2019. Publications. Newberry.Org. publications.newberry.org/digitalexhibitions/exhibits/show/realizingthenewberryidea/researchteachingpublishing/butlers.

"Sam Houston Biography & Facts." Encyclopedia Britannica. 2019. www.britannica.com/biography/Sam-Houston.

"Texas 175: A Dozen Documents that Made a Difference." 2019. Texas State Library and Archives. www.tsl.texas.gov/exhibits/texas175/emilywest.html.

"Transcript of Obligation of Indenture Binding Nancy Ann Morgan to James Morgan, April 28, 1834." The Portal to Texas History. texashistory.unt.edu/ark:/67531/metapth218106/?q=james%20morgan.

WBAP-TV (television station, Fort Worth, TX). News Script: Mitch Miller, item, August 16, 1955; University of North Texas Libraries, Digital Library, crediting UNT Libraries Special Collections. digital.library.unt.edu/ark:/67531/metadc778120/m1/1.

Whiteford, R., and L.S. Punderson. "Map of the City of New Haven, from Surveys, 1852." New Haven Free Public Library Digital Collections. nhfpl.omeka.net/items/show/848.

"William Bollaert Notes and Memoranda, 1837–1838." Edward E. Ayer Digital Collection (Newberry Library). collections.carli.illinois.edu/cdm/ref/collection/nby_eeayer/id/65227.

Lectures and Interviews

Bailey, Michael. Personal interview. Houston, April 3, 2019.

Fowler, William C. "The Historical Status of the Negro in Connecticut. A Paper Read before the New Haven Colony Historical Society." Presentation, New Haven, CT, 1900.

Houston, Sam. "Speech of General Sam Houston of Texas Refuting Calumnies Produced and Circulated Against His Character as Commander-in-Chief of the Army of Texas; Delivered in the Senate of the United States, February 28, 1859." Washington, D.C.

Parsley, Jennifer. Personal interview. Houston, April 22, 2019.

Journals and Dissertations

Baker, Eugene. "The San Jacinto Campaign." *Quarterly of the Texas State Historical Association* 4, no. 4 (April 1901): 237–345.

Belton, John. "The Searchers: Essays and Reflections on John Ford's Classic Western." *Film Quarterly* 59, no. 3 (2006): 80–82. doi:10.1525/fq.2006.59.3.80.

Bryant, D.L. "Emily D. West and the Yellow Rose of Texas Myth." *Choice* 52, no. 4 (2014): 687–88. search.proquest.com.ezp-prod1.hul.harvard.edu/docview/1646887148?accountid=11311.

Klein, Herbert S. "The English Slave Trade to Jamaica, 1782–1808." *Economic History Review* 31, no. 1 (1978): 25–45. doi:10.2307/2595799.

Lundy, Benjamin. "Genius of Universal Emancipation." *Genius Emancipation* 1, no. 3 (1833).

Marble, Earl, ed. *FOLIO: A Journal of Music, Art, Drama and Literature* 21, no. 1 (1882): 130–31.

Martin, Scott C. "Interpreting 'Metamora': Nationalism, Theater, and Jacksonian Indian Policy." *Journal of the Early Republic* 19, no. 1 (1999): 73–101. doi:10.2307/3124923.

Menschel, David. "Abolition without Deliverance: The Law of Connecticut Slavery 1784–1848." *Yale Law Journal* 111, no. 1 (2001). www.yalelawjournal.org/note/abolition-without-deliverance-the-law-of-connecticut-slavery-1784-1848.

Rosen, Bruce. "Abolition and Colonization, the Years of Conflict: 1829–1834." *Phylon* 33, no. 2 (1972): 177–92. doi:10.2307/273347.

Schmitz, Joseph William. "Social Conditions in the Republic of Texas, 1836–1845." Master's diss., Loyola University, 1934. ecommons.luc.edu/luc_theses/363.

Schoen, Harold. "The Free Negro in the Republic of Texas, IV." *Southwestern Historical Quarterly* 40, no. 3 (1937): 169–99. www.jstor.org/stable/30235617.

Spence, Mary Lee. "British Impressions of Texas and the Texans." *Southwestern Historical Quarterly* 70, no. 2 (1966): 163–83. www.jstor.org/stable/30236385.

Stewart, James Brewer. "The New Haven Negro College and the Meanings of Race in New England, 1776–1870." *New England Quarterly* 76, no. 3 (2003): 323–55. doi:10.2307/1559806.

Winters, James Washington. "An Account of the Battle of San Jacinto." *Quarterly of the Texas State Historical Association* 6, no. 2 (1902): 139–44.

Magazines and News Articles

AP News. "Historian Disputes Legend of Yellow Rose of Texas." November 7, 1985. apnews.com/e5e8544c12be59532cb495169062a39c.

Gan, Vicky. "The Story Behind the Failed Minstrel Show at the 1964 World's Fair." *Smithsonian*, April 28, 2014. www.smithsonianmag.com/history/minstrel-show-1964-worlds-fair-180951239.

Hallman, Tristan. "Dallas' Robert E. Lee Park Officially Renamed Oak Lawn Park—For Now; Task Force Recommends More Removals." Dallasnews.Com, September 2019. www.dallasnews.com/news/dallas-city-hall/2017/09/22/dallas-robert-e-lee-park-officially-renamed-oak-lawn-park-now.

Harrigan, Steve. "Texas Primer: The Yellow Rose of Texas." *Texas Monthly*, April 1984. www.texasmonthly.com/the-culture/texas-primer-the-yellow-rose-of-texas.

Holley, Joe. "Mystery Still Surrounds 'Yellow Rose of Texas.'" Houstonchronicle.com, April 1, 2016. www.houstonchronicle.com/news/columnists/native-texan/article/Mystery-still-surrounds-Yellow-Rose-of-Texas-7222989.php.

Iinuma, Kevin. "Command Chief's Spouse Receives Yellow Rose of Texas Award." *59th Medical Wing*, June 22, 2012. www.59mdw.af.mil/News/Article-Display/Article/407427/command-chiefs-spouse-receives-yellow-rose-of-texas-award.

Lindsay, Tom. "After Public Backlash, Texas Education Will Continue to Remember the Alamo." Forbes.com, September 20, 2018. www.forbes.com/sites/tomlindsay/2018/09/20/after-public-backlash-texas-education-will-continue-to-remember-the-alamo/#13db0cdf5472.

Soodalter, Ron. "The Strangest Adoption in the History of the West." *True West Magazine*, September 12, 2016. truewestmagazine.com/the-strangest-adoption-in-the-history-of-the-west.

Staples, Brent. "Manhattan Minstrel Show." Nytimes.com, October 13, 1993. www.nytimes.com/1993/10/13/opinion/manhattan-minstrel-show.html.

Taylor, Lonn. "Santa Anna's Chamber Pot." *Texas Monthly*, 2014. www.texasmonthly.com/the-culture/santa-annas-chamber-pot.

Tyler Morning Telegraph. "Maymerle Brown." June 2, 2017. obituaries.tylerpaper.com/obituaries/tylerpaper/obituary.aspx?n=maymerle-shirley-brown&pid=185701583.

Wallace, Christian. "Texas, My Texas, You Deserve a New State Song." *Texas Monthly*, 2016. www.texasmonthly.com/the-culture/texas-my-texas-you-deserve-a-new-state-song.

Weber, Andrew. "Passports Required for Traveling into and out of the Republic of Texas." Kut.org, 2019. www.kut.org/post/passports-required-traveling-and-out-republic-texas.

Poems and Essays

Abernethy, F.E., and Shannon Thompson, eds. "The Elusive Emily West, Folksong's Fabled 'Yellow Rose of Texas.'" In *2001: A Texas Folklore Odyssey*. Denton, University of North Texas, 2001.

Jones, Jim, and Jean Elizabeth Ward, eds. "Emily West of Morgan's Point." In *Black Pioneer*, 2010, 131. www.lulu.com.

Websites

"Auction 4: Lots 173–188." Dsloan.com, 2019. www.dsloan.com/Auctions/a4/Lots_173-188.html.

"Billboard Top 100." HowdyYall.com. howdyyall.com/Texas/TodaysNews/index.cfm?DisplayDay=24&DisplayMonth=8.

Blight, David, and Paul Lawrence. "Citizens ALL: African Americans in Connecticut 1700–1850." The Gilder Lehrman Center for the Study of Slavery, Resistance, and Abolition. glc.yale.edu/citizens/about.

"The Boston Riot of 1835." Teachushistory.org. www.teachushistory.org/second-great-awakening-age-reform/resources/boston-riot-1835.

"British and French Prisoners of War, 1793–1815." Royal Museums Greenwich, UNESCO World Heritage Site, 2017. www.rmg.co.uk/discover/behind-the-scenes/blog/british-and-french-prisoners-war-1793-1815.

Connor, Seymour V. "New Washington, Tx." Handbook of Texas Online. www.tshaonline.org/handbook/online/articles/hvn28.

Covington, Carolyn Callaway. "Runaway Scrape." Handbook of Texas Online. www.tshaonline.org/handbook/online/articles/pfr01.

Dall, Curtis B. "Holley, Mary Austin." Handbook of Texas Online. www.tshaonline.org/handbook/online/articles/fho32.

Dean, Lynn. "Road to Revolution: The Yellow Rose of Texas." Discover Texas, 2017. www.discovertexasonline.com/2017/04/road-to-revolution-the-yellow-rose-of-texas.

Deeringer, Martha. "Santa Anna's Complex Character." Texas Co-Op Power Magazine, April 2015. www.texascooppower.com/texas-stories/history/santa-annas-complex-character.

Dunn, Jeffrey D., and James Lutzweiler. "Yellow Rose of Texas." Handbook of Texas Online. www.tshaonline.org/handbook/online/articles/xey01.

"1834 Anti-Abolitionist Riots." Build Nation. 2016. buildnationblog. wordpress.com/2016/03/09/1834-anti-abolitionist-riots.

"The Equal Rights Amendment." www.equalrightsamendment.org/the-equal-rights-amendment.

"Foster—Song of America." 1826. songofamerica.net/composer/foster-stephen.

Harris, Leslie. "Newsletter—African-Americans." Emory University Department of History, August 2001. history.emory.edu/newsletter01/newsl01/african.htm.

Harss, Marina. "Donald Byrd and Spectrum Dance Theater—The Minstrel Show Revisited—New York." Dancetabs, 2015. dancetabs. com/2015/11/donald-byrd-and-spectrum-dance-theater-the-minstrel-show-revisited-new-york.

Hazlewood, Claudia. "Archives War." Handbook of Texas Online. www. tshaonline.org/handbook/online/articles/mqa02.

Henson, Margaret Swett. "Burnet, David Gouverneur." Handbook of Texas Online. www.tshaonline.org/handbook/online/articles/fbu46.

———. "West, Emily D." Handbook of Texas Online. www.tshaonline.org/handbook/online/articles/fwe41.

Kirk, Elise. "Music in Lincoln's White House." White House Historical Association. www.whitehousehistory.org/music-in-lincolns-white-house.

Lutzweiler, James. "The Believability of William Bollaert's Story about Santa Anna and His Revolutionary Rendezvous with Emily D. West at San Jacinto on 21 April 1836." www.sonsofdewittcolony.org/lutzweiler.pdf.

McGowan, Shane. "Will You Come to the Bower?" Irish Music Daily, 2013. /www.irishmusicdaily.com/will-you-come-to-the-bower.

Melish, Joanne Pope. "Background—Slavery in New England." Deerfield History Museum. 1704.deerfield.history.museum/popups/background. do?shortName=expSlavery.

Miller, Jonnie. "Runaway Scrape—The Hidden Event of the Texas Revolution." Center for Regional Heritage Research. Sfasu.edu, May 2018. www.sfasu.edu/heritagecenter/991.

"Prisoners and Detainees in War." Europäische Geschichte Online, 2019. ieg-ego.eu/en/threads/alliances-and-wars/war-as-an-agent-of-transfer/sibylle-scheipers-prisoners-and-detainees-in-war.

"Runaway Scrape." Wikipedia.org. en.wikipedia.org/wiki/Runaway_Scrape#cite_ref-Scrape_43-0.

Sibley, Marilyn M. "Lundy, Benjamin." Handbook of Texas Online. www.tshaonline.org/handbook/online/articles/flu10.

"Snow Riot." Wikipedia.org. en.wikipedia.org/wiki/Snow_Riot.

"Susanna Dickinson." Sons of deWitt Colony. www.sonsofdewittcolony.org//adp/history/bios/dickenson/dickinson_susannah.html.

"The U.S.-Mexican War (1846–1848)." Pbs.org, 2019. www.pbs.org/kera/usmexicanwar.

Index

About the Author

Texas author and storyteller Lora-Marie Bernard writes nonfiction books that look at historic Lone Star stories through a modern lens.

Her family lived in Burleson, Texas, near Fort Worth. Her mother was a German immigrant, and her father was a first-generation Italian American. They raised her and her brother with small-town Texas values and international mindsets.

Her father told her Texas was going to be one of the most prosperous states in the nation for the rest of her life. She believed him. Educated in the "Texas state of mind," she never questioned that she'd spend her life telling the stories about the state and the people who make its past, present and future.

From Fort Worth, she moved to the Greater Houston/Galveston region and lived on the Texas island for several years. It was on the southeast coastal prairies that she became an award-winning journalist and storyteller.

For decades, she was a newsroom reporter, where she won numerous Associated Press awards and national press honors for her public affairs and investigative reporting. She continues to serve as a radio commentator and news correspondent on Texas issues for national media outlets. She covered President Donald J. Trump's nomination at the 2016 Republican National Convention, his Texas presidential campaign and the 2017 inauguration.

Other national correspondence coverage also includes the Women's March in Washington, D.C., Hurricane Harvey and the U.S. Senate race between Ted Cruz and Beto O'Rourke.

She earned her master's degree in liberal arts extension studies at Harvard University. She concentrated in journalism and museum studies. Her undergraduate degree is from the Mayborn School of Journalism at the University of North Texas. She heads a media and outreach consulting firm in Houston.

Other books by Lora-Marie include *Lower Brazos River Canals*, *Houston Center: A Vision to Excellence* and *Counterfeit Prince of Old Texas: Slaving Swindler Monroe Edwards*.

Visit us at
www.historypress.com